ACT

LIKE A

GENTLEMAN

THINK

LIKE A

WOMAN

ACT LIKE A GENTLEMAN, THINK LIKE A WOMAN:

a Woman's Response to Steve Harvey's
Act Like a Lady, Think Like a Man

MARIA BUSTILLOS

Accidental Books
Los Angeles

For Oliver

CONTENTS

Audire est operae pretium, procedere recte
qui moechos non vultis, ut omni parte laborent;
utque illis multo corrupta dolore voluptas,
atque haec rara cadat dura inter saepe pericla.

HORACE, *Satires.*

PREFACE

The book *Act Like a Lady, Think Like a Man* is a very popular how-to guide for helping women "get" and "keep" a Man. Its author, Steve Harvey, is convinced that single women are going about securing a man the wrong way, and he has come along to guide them, so that they can Get That Man, finally. It has chapters called "How to Get the Ring," and "Why Men Cheat," and the final section of his book is called "The Playbook: How to Win the Game."

Mr. Harvey has got a friendly, aw-shucks image it is impossible to dislike, even if you don't quite go along with the idea that what all women want is to Get a Man. I'm sure, too, that there must be a lot of single women in the position he describes: lacking in confidence, or lonely, and letting their menfolk call all the shots out of sheer desperation. But as I read this book, I couldn't help but think that what is equally, not to say blindingly, evident is the fact that there are quite a lot of lonely, frustrated guys out there, too. At least as many, surely. After all, who has to pay to get into the nightclubs? Who is being spammed to kingdom come with offers of genital enlargement? Who is shopping for picture brides? Who is eating all this Viagra?

Not women!

To hear Mr. Harvey tell it, men are just a bunch of naughty tomcats who need to be brought into line by their tough-lovin' women, and then everybody is going to be happy. This theory is very hard to buy. For starters, I can't believe that men are so brainless as to need a list of demands from women (what Mr. Harvey calls "standards" regarding fidelity and so on) in order to act in a principled way. And then, there are so many unhappy men out there whose women are *already* bossing them around; there's a horrible name for that. Hasn't Mr. Harvey got the wrong end of the whip, I thought? By the time I'd finished his book, I was sure that he had indeed. At least half the real story was not being told, and fair play demanded a response.

I have long felt the same kind of pity and distress

on behalf of lonely, misguided men as Mr. Harvey appears to feel on behalf of frustrated women. He claims to be aiding women by telling them all about the secrets of men, so that they can get what they want ("the Ring," etc.) from them. Surely it is only fair that a sympathetic woman should do men the same favor, and divulge all *our* secrets to *them*: and I am that woman.

The advice commonly given by men, to men on the subject of courting women is nothing short of catastrophic. One angry-looking "expert" can, at the time of this writing, be found on YouTube giving men who want to "attract younger women" such pointers as "Nice Guy Must Die" (he means stop acting like one, apparently,) "be confident," and wear a red tie, because "it's a phallic symbol." Not content with merely fleecing these lonely guys, this fellow also contrives to send them headlong in the wrong direction. It's heartbreaking, really.

So this book was written by a woman, for men, in answer to Mr. Harvey's book. It reveals all our secrets, so that men, too, can get what they want from women—which, as I understand it, is to get them into bed.

If you want to shoot the lion, by all means you may ask the hunter how to go about it (having first ascertained that he has, in fact, actually shot one.) But better still, if you can, you should ask the *lion* how to shoot the lion. Naturally, it is a very wicked lion who

*Klaus Fuchs ID badge
from Los Alamos,
via Wikimedia Commons*

will tell. A really bad lioness like myself finds herself in rather the position of Klaus Fuchs, a fellow betrayer for the greater good. Like Fuchs, I am in possession of valuable secret knowledge that I am convinced the other side has a right to. This is a question not only of fairness, but of maintaining the great equilibrium that transcends us all. Surely, neither hunter nor lion should ever have the upper hand completely; the law of the jungle must be kept in balance, for everyone's sake.

Therefore, in the following pages I will reveal to you the deepest workings of the female mind; I will betray to you all our secrets in such detail you will never be insecure about your ability to attract a woman again. Yes! I am going to tell you all you need to know in order to get exactly what you want, which is to get laid. (I will also tell you a whole lot of other things about women that you are probably less interested in, but just in case.)

It's so very simple, you won't believe it. I will be assuming at the outset, of course, that all you want is the one thing. I won't be crediting you with any kind of conscience, nor scruples, nor any desire to actually get to know women as individuals and human beings. Nope! Just as all women are after "the Ring," apparently, so are you men every bit as hell-bent on getting laid without having to produce one. And I am going to tell you exactly how to achieve this.

Everything You Need to Know About Women is Right Here.

I've talked to a lot of lovelorn men in my time. Not, it is true, on a radio show, like Mr. Harvey, but just in the ordinary course of an eventful and garrulous life. And I have found that these men say the same thing over and over again: they don't understand women.

Many is the time I have found myself perplexed when I consider that all these men, who have obviously run across at least a few women and are consequently in a position to observe exactly what makes them tick, *still* cannot seem to manage to obtain the mindless sex they say they need and want. Women, however desirable, are as a sealéd book to them. How, they endlessly wonder, can they manage to get into the pants of women?

Fortunately, I have been able to share and refine my wisdom—wisdom gained from decades of being a woman myself—in talking with (and particularly, in listening to) a lot of men. I have also yapped forever with my friends who are, like myself, women, and well known to be brimful of opinions on the topic of men. One of the most important things I have learned is that we women are not as "complicated" as we are painted, not by a long chalk. Women—quite a number of them, anyway—pretty much want all the same things, all of them, all the time. They will respond to the same stimuli in the same way, like a giant pack of several billion Pavlov's dogs. Complications may present themselves but even so, we women are equipped with certain basic features that men can very easily learn about and exploit. Very easily! You will observe how very short a book this is ... that's right, chaps, an undeceived approach to the simple facts can get you right where you want to go. Do I advise this approach? Please understand, this is not a work of philosophy or ethics; I'm just explaining to you how women think and operate; after that you can make up your own mind as to how to conduct yourself.

I do believe, though, that both men and women will be better served if we all just say exactly what it is we are up to right up front, and not dress it all up in code words like "commitment" and "gold-digger" and "tease" and "playa" and all that. To that extent, Mr. Harvey and I are in perfect accord.

Like Mr. H., I understand that some women are so selfish and so desperate to "Get the Ring" and be married that they are will force men to put up with all kinds of crazy stuff like 500-person guest lists and piles of fabric swatches and horribly awkward family obligations, etc. Like him, I understand that men are desperate for sex, and though they will do most anything that women demand in order to get it, they quite often balk at the idea of marriage. You'd think it would be impossible to reconcile these two positions, but the chasm between them is negotiated between us every day, however clumsily and ineffectively. This book will give you all the tools you need in order to traverse that eternal divide like Jean-Claude Killy barreling down La Face at Val d'Isère.

So please forget everything you think you know about women. Everything your friends have said, all those expensive audio tapes about How to Get Any Woman to Sleep With You, grotesque advice regarding ties, everything you've read in *Playboy, GQ* and *Maxim.* I want you to understand the tactics and mindset of women so that you can get what you want, *without being played yourself.*

Using this book, you'll be able to understand the basic structure of a woman's character, anticipate her every move, and use that information to get her into bed with no strings attached. As I said earlier, I doubt you care since y'all are only interested in the one thing, but using this book, you'll also be able to learn all sorts of other, different kinds of things about women that may eventually come in handy, too. So, here we go. In order to get what you want from women, you must:

Act like a gentleman, and think like a woman.

MISINFORMATION

I'll bet you've got this idea of a man who is likely to do well with women. Rich, tall, muscular, spends a lot of time at the gym. Makes a lot of money and drives a flash car. Smart too, no doubt, "successful." He probably has other James-Bondish features as well; knows a lot about wine, dresses well, speaks two or three languages, well-traveled.

How can anyone compete with such a paragon? Clearly the only thing for the ordinary man to do is throw up his hands in despair and hope he can somehow attract the company of some bedraggled and cut-rate but halfway willing female, while the so-called paragons make off with all the fine women. Right?

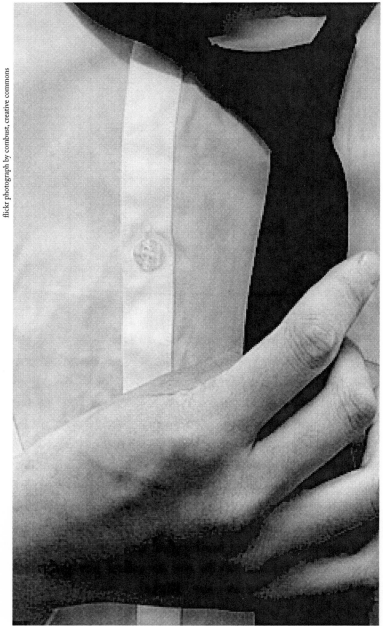

Everything, literally everything you are thinking here is false. I don't know where these delusional James Bond fantasy figures come from (though I suspect they are transmitted mainly via the distilled insecurities of male screenwriters,) but it's all *wrong*. To begin with (and please remember, you're hearing this from a woman,) what women really think of overachieving self-infatuated guys who drive embarrassingly ostentatious cars and spend half the day adoring their own reflections in the gym, you know, well—we think they are liable to be absolute tools. We assume: *this guy probably thinks he'd be doing me a big favor by asking me out—gross!*

Even if such a guy is not really a big poser, but only "successful," as in super career-driven, the average woman is liable to think: *he'll never be home; he's too busy for me; I'll be forever waiting by the telephone. I'll never come first with him.* If we are not really materialists ourselves, a guy with too much money is apt to kind of scare us off, too. We worry that he won't like our friends, or like going to our favorite hole in the wall; that we will wind up stuck in some stultifying Four Seasons hotel all day while he goes and plays golf with a load of total creeps. And, worst of all: how many other women is this guy paying court to? Am I going to be just no. 8? Is this one of those Hefner scenarios because if it is, in the wise words of Sam Goldwyn, include me out.

So, in order to get girls into bed quite easily, does a man need to be rich? No.

Muscular? Certainly not.

"Successful?" No.

Giant penis? NO.

Fancy car? Don't make me laugh!

All these absurd ideas about being a hit with chicks came not from women but from *men*, and still worse, from men who have absolutely *no idea* how women are constituted.

So first of all, you've got to clear your mind completely of every preconception you've been fed about women and what they want from men.

Let me begin by setting you straight on the main point:

It's not about you; it's about her.

LAID

So, gentlemen. Everyone knows how wonderful the Love of a Good Woman is. It can rescue anybody from disaster, it can mend a broken character, it can fix everything that has ever gone wrong in your life. Probably! So that is what you want, right? The Love of a Good Woman?

No?

You just want to get off.

But look, now. Men come to value the stability and warmth that a good family life can give them. A real home to come home to, not some squalid, miserable sterile bachelor pad with sheets that haven't been changed in six months and nothing in the refrigerator except an ancient dried-up piece of cheese, a packet of

Tyranov, *Young Housewife*, via Wikimedia Commons

Domestic goddess ca. 1840

soy sauce and some beer. A real home is an environment that is calm, welcoming and orderly. There will be fresh flowers around, stuff for snacks. It's a place where you can invite your friends and business associates and know they'll be well taken care of, with good wine and food and jokes and lovely furnishings and fun, and everything that can encourage people to feel happy, comfortable and welcome. Most of all, someone who loves you is there waiting for you, someone who is so glad you're home.

No?

Just sex, eh? Well! So I've heard ... Hmm.

When things go wrong at work, or if you get a speeding ticket, or if you lose your job, or you get sick, it is very nice to have a smart, loyal and loving companion to look out for you. She can make you laugh, make sure you don't ever get too low. She will tell you that she knows you are brilliant and talented and that you are a good man, and she'll be able to tell you so you can actually believe it, because *she* does. When you've got a plan for a new business or project, a good companion is invaluable, can strengthen you in so many ways. You know one another so well, have been through so much together. Francis Bacon's remark regarding the value of a friend applies even more truly to a companion in life, a mate: "For there is no man, that imparteth his joys to his friend, but he joyeth the more; and no man that imparteth his griefs to his friend, but he grieveth the less."

No!! Okay!! I get it. You (or quite a lot of you, I guess) are only interested in the sex.

Please forget everything I just said, then. You don't need to demonstrate intelligence, affection, conscience, constancy, a sense of responsibility, or any of that.

Men Who Want an Actual Relationship:
Please Skip the Following Section, Because it is Only
for Men Who Want to Get Laid
and That is It.

Here are the attributes that you need to look for in a woman in order to get her into bed with a minimum of fuss and virtually no need to phone her afterward, if you don't feel like it, but you'll most likely still be able to call her back at any time and return to her bed at will. This woman will need to be:

1. Beautiful.
2. Dumb.
3. The more self-esteem issues, the better.

Beautiful.

You'll doubtless be surprised and thrilled to hear that beautiful women are in fact by far the easiest to get into bed. Why? Because beautiful women live and die by their beauty. Those women who spend hours primping and working out and having their hair and nails seen to, who cannot eat one cornflake without freaking out, who fuss and worry themselves obsessively over every imaginary, impending or potential flaw—these women are going through such an insane amount of effort for just one reason: in order for you to find them beautiful. Indeed, if nobody admires a beautiful woman, she ceases to be beautiful. Admiration is the very air they are breathing. This is their weakness, their Achilles' heel. If you take pains to admire such a woman, you have already won half the battle by providing her with the fuel she needs in order to maintain her fragile, dependent self-image.

Proceed, then, to take advantage of this weakness by flattering that beautiful woman to hell and back. You can never do this blatantly enough. There will never be enough flattery and it can never be too absurdly exaggerated. Provided you are not a complete troglodyte, even a wolf-whistle from across the street generally constitutes welcome attention to a beautiful woman. Telling her that her eyes are haunting you, that her perfume drives you wild, that you think of her every moment you are awake and dream of her every night as you sleep—this is the kind of stuff to lay on with a trowel. Especially if the woman in question is:

Dumb.

I will be blunt. You are looking for sex and you didn't specify that it had to be meaningful or fascinating; you don't care about the quality of the experience that comes before or after; you are looking to get laid. Okay! Find the dumbest most beautiful woman you possibly can, and you're almost home. If she is seriously dumb, this beautiful woman will NEVER stop to think why on earth you are saying and doing all these wonderful things on her behalf. She won't be concerned about a future, and she doesn't care about clever conversation any more than you do, right? She wouldn't know clever conversation if it hit her on the head with a brick, and so much the better for you. It will more than suffice that you opened the door of the car for her, that you pulled out her chair, that you ordered her drink for her. Wow, she is thinking. This is the real deal!

Please note that it is not necessary for any of this stuff to be particularly costly. It's just as pleasing to a woman (even a smart one, truth to tell) whether the drink you ordered for her is a beer or a wonderful Sancerre, provided you know it's something she really likes.

If she is really, really dumb, it simply will not occur to her that this gravy train of attention and concern will come to a screeching halt whenever you want. If she is straight-up stupid, she'll agree to meet you again, and again, even after you haven't called her back for one month and now you feel like getting laid and you apply the soft soap about how beautiful her legs are and how you can't wait to feel them wrapped around you etc. etc.

So the dumber, the better.

Self-esteem issues.

A very insecure woman is a creature of needs. She needs to hear that someone—practically anyone—finds her interesting, pretty, attractive and desirable. She needs attention; she craves company; she doesn't want to be alone. She is a mess! But you don't care about that because what you want is to get laid. This is just the girl for you.

When a girl has no self-esteem whatsoever, she's like a sort of vacuum for flattery. She will buy the most impossible, outrageous praise without raising a single meticulously-tweezed eyebrow. You can tell her that she should get a Nobel Prize or the Fields Medal and she will believe you, because there's nothing in her head or heart but an insatiable need to hear something good about herself. Is this sad, well yeah, kind of but do you care?! No!! You said so earlier. It's all booty call, friends with benefits no strings rocks off! Okay then.

Tell her how beautiful she is, how arresting. Oh, go ahead and tell her you've become obsessed with her. You can lie because you don't care! You want to get off, so that's what you say.

Oh wait, though; I was asking you to be a gentleman, earlier—to be considerate, kind, truthful? No indeed not at all, if all you want is to have sex, and that is it. Not necessary. Just *act* like a gentleman, as the title of this book proposes. Provide a reasonable facsimile there-of. If our girl is sufficiently dumb and desperate, that will be more than enough for her. (We'll be spending some time with this unfortunate female; what shall we call her? I know! How about "Patsy"?)

I mean, take it either way. You can really *be* a gentleman, or you can just act like one, depending on where you're going with your goals, here. I'm just illu-minating the real conditions in which men and women are conducting their weird *pas de deux* as they have for probably tens of thousands of years running. I'm telling you the real reality of how women operate, what makes us tick.

What's that you say? You think that a real gentle-man should actually mean it when he buys a girl a drink, at least just out of common kindness? You think that a man who produces the form of consideration without its substance is basically a cad, do you? Well ... as I was say-ing earlier, this is not really a book of moral philosophy (and I'm not exactly John Stuart Mill.) I'm not about to get into any of that here.

TOUGH EGGS

N ow that you know your chances are best with a woman who is beautiful, dumb, and low on self-esteem, let's go over a few details regarding women who fall outside these parameters. What if the woman of your dreams is beautiful and also smart? Not great-looking but witty and fun, with a sardonic sense of humor? These are the tough eggs, and far harder to crack; let's see what we can do about them.

First, please consider some elementary facts about female psychology. We know that you want to sleep with women. The question is, how do they feel about sleeping with you? In the beginning, I mean, before you have begun your campaign. Well, one thing we can say without reservation is this: a woman may not want to sleep with you to begin with, but she most certainly wants *you* to want to sleep with *her*. Or more accurately, she naturally *assumes* that you want to, right from the beginning, and something must be seriously wrong if you don't. Now, don't be alarmed by the fact that women feel this way, because there isn't a woman on this earth who doesn't prefer to be desired than not; you can take that to the bank.

Please understand, we feel this way not because *we* are so undiscriminating, but because *y'all* are. It's a given for most of us that every man we see would like to sleep with us, if he could, right now. There is ample evidence of this, frankly. One observes from a very early age that all men seem to want to, all the time, all men, all of them, all men of pretty much every age and description; and they certainly do not seem to be terribly particular about who with. So it stands to reason that unless we are very very unattractive indeed, as in hideous, unwashed toothless hags of ninety, most men would absolutely pounce if given the chance. To that extent, we are onto you.

Even though most men appear to want to sleep with us, though, it doesn't mean a thing, because they also want to sleep with every other female they see. Big deal! It's nothing special, it's just the law of the jungle. No female with any sense at all attaches much importance to it (see "Dumb," above.) Only today I was leaving stuff off at a thrift shop and some egregious young pup scarcely old enough to shave came up and asked me for my phone number, if you can believe, and I am only a very nice middle-aged lady. "You look good, kitty-cat!" he observed myopically. "Can I have your number?"

Poor kid was probably stoned out of his mind, but still. Did I mind? Absurd as it is I confess to you that no, even at my advanced age, and knowing all that I do, I did *not* really mind, I guess because it was a genial, if wacky, reminder that I am not yet toothless, unwashed and ninety. Most women, like me, hear such stuff and similarly think oh, *whatever.* (And no, I did not give him my number! Good grief.)

So anyway, we were determining whether women want to sleep with you (a critical point.) Here we come to a second fact about female psychology. Women operate in exactly *the opposite way from men.* Just as men automatically want to sleep with more or less every woman they see, and the door for them is almost always open, in women the door is set to "closed" as the default position. For obvious reasons. If women, also, were naturally set to "open," none of us would ever accomplish anything at all, and civilization would collapse. Obviously, one of the two sexes must be turned to Off; and in the case of our species (and that of hamsters, as we shall see) it is the females who thus prevent the collapse of civilization.

Eventually, the door may open; a woman may privately consider opening it quite early in the proceedings. She will be kind of weighing what conditions would be required for opening the door. She might like to make sure that you are kind, for example, affectionate, amusing. She might just want to verify that you are not going to be like that one maniac of a boyfriend she had, who set fire to the curtains and had to be hauled off by the fuzz. The door may just spring open all of a sudden, really, almost unconsciously, without her knowing it, even. Or she may make a great show of putting a padlock on there, in your presence. That is not a good sign, but even then it could indicate a protracted siege, rather than a permanent state of affairs.

Be aware, however, that it is not at all uncommon to find that No means No. You'd do better to cut your losses and find a more promising specimen, if the resistance looks like it's going to be on the hard side. Decide how much effort you want to put into the courtship, right at the outset if you can.

What I am getting at is this: for the quickest and easiest results, it is of the utmost importance to choose your prey wisely. While the advice I am about to give you may eventually bring home the bacon in any case, what we're aiming for here is efficiency. (Being a man, of course, you are liable to have let your libido get the better of you already, and you already have a specific woman in mind as you read this book. That is okay, we will see what we can do.)

I understand that you may even *prefer* a bit of a challenge: fair enough. Despite their general lack of discrimination, most men appear to feel that the "fast" female is not the choicest. Maybe because you are supposing that they are out for what they can get from you? Or maybe it is the fact that nobody cares for what is too common, and has already been distributed far and wide like so many supermarket coupons. Opinions vary here, I have noticed. I once knew an old gentleman who was a great admirer of fast women.

"They're not *loose!*" he declared firmly. "I always thought they were *generous.*"

There is certainly something in that.

To be sure, attraction is a notoriously difficult thing to control. Nevertheless, you might consider the following before we move on. Given that your intentions are basically lustful, there are several types of women you really ought to at least try to avoid entirely.

Women With Clipboards

Steve Harvey seems to think that women should be *very* demanding; in fact, he has an actual list of things they

Josephine Baker in 1927; photo by Walery via Wikimedia Commons

GENEROUS.

should demand to know from men, right up front. It's like, *instructions.* He advises women to sort of "interview" the men they are dating with these specific questions, very early on. I shudder to think that anybody would subject another person, man or woman, to this horrific interrogation, which includes "short- and long-term plans," personal relationships ("what is his relationship with his mother?") and finally, "What do you think of me?" and "How do you feel about me?"

If anybody were to let me in for a grilling like that, there is no way on earth I could ever be persuaded to go on another date. In this instance, the classic advice about not "coming on too strong" is beyond right. I cannot imagine that that hideous Perry Mason routine wouldn't send any halfway sane man running headlong in the opposite direction.

And it *should*, is what I am telling you.

If a woman opens the proceedings by giving you the third degree, or by being too needy and/or too panicky, it is likely going to be a *huge* amount of trouble to get her into bed. Not even getting into the fact that it is going to be tough even to enjoy her company at all freely, when she's holding up some kind of unholy scorecard up at you all the time. A date should never be a job interview for the position of Boyfriend or Husband. It's some time you spend together in order to hang out for a while, have fun, and maybe get to know one another better. Find someone who is capable of that, if possible.

Spoiled Brats: Stay Away

There are loads of women who have been advised that what they need to be doing is finding a man who cares only and absolutely about them, to the total exclusion of all else, and they have been crazy enough to swallow that Kool-Aid. Such women require proof of absolute, groveling devotion at all times in the form of gifts, unending flattery, fancy evenings out, birthday surprises and the like.

I know this one married guy whose home life is conducted in an ongoing state of panic, rising to abject terror at holidays. When Christmas rolls around he doesn't know what to buy, but he does know that he had better show up with a whole bunch of stuff or there will be hell to pay; he doesn't want to go to any danged mall, but he is in terrible fear of the showdown there will be if he doesn't. So Christmas Eve he rushes all around the mall like a wild man, blindly slamming stuff, anything practically, into shopping carts (much of which, incidentally, he will have to return later.) This goes on year after year. Many a sitcom has been predicated on the comedy value of the terror-shopping exercise, but I really don't think anyone finds it so funny when he or she is one of the principals.

This unfortunate soul also complains that he does not get laid often enough. I can imagine nothing more humiliating than feeling that one is being "given" sex as a "favor," which is how it often goes with the spoiled brats. Listen. You don't have to put up with any of that for one second, and you really shouldn't, either.

Being terrified into paying attention to someone as a means of avoiding unpleasantness is *not* the same as an ordinary demonstration of appreciation. Be on the lookout for women who have that air of tyranny about them, who are quick to throw a hissy or otherwise punish you if you should fall short of their expectations in some small way. Such women are so self-involved that they are poor dissimulators, have no impulse control and cannot govern their unreasonable tempers, so they are easy to spot.

Smart Women: The Bad News

I am sorry to have to break this to you, but there is no magical way to make an ordinary, intelligent woman turn into a sex-crazed pole-dancer.

Here's the main difficulty. Intelligent, together women are constituted to wait for the irresistible signal from their *own* bodies in order to want to make love with you. That is to say, they can't be talked into it just because *you* want to. The signal comes from *them*, not from you. No, not even if you have an absolutely monstrous penis! They have to really want to, themselves, for themselves. It takes a woman who suffers from really deep-seated insecurities to agree to the so-called "mindless" sex at all promptly. In short, the less insecure they are, the harder it will be to cajole them into bed.

Smart women just have to want to on their own, because you are beautiful, and you have been good to them and you have fascinated and seduced them, and they have seduced you back. For their own purposes, because you have amused and attracted them, they like the idea of hanging around with you, and they like the idea of becoming intimate with you. Hence, and please take heed, such women are not really the subject of this book. If you have fallen for one of these women, I'm afraid you're going to have to take your time; though my advice will still be worth reading, there are definite limits to the miracles I can work for you.

The Good News: the Myth of Independent Women

We need one another, and that is a good thing. Whoever is really completely independent and doesn't need other people for anything at any time is a sociopath, and consequently not admirable or enviable in any way. Such a person is on the contrary to be pitied from the bottom of our hearts.

This is another area where I am in perfect agreement with Mr. Harvey, who thinks that women who are in a big old hurry to show men how independent they are (by paying their half of the check, and/or scorning having the door opened and stuff) are really making a hash of things. It is okay to need one another. It's the truth! We *do* need one another. Things will go better if we just acknowledge that from the start, as the wise old Cocktail Era did.

I disagree entirely with Mr. Harvey, however, that being a lady means "having standards" such as demanding that whatever guy give you flowers, or hold a chair for you. Being a lady means being thoughtful to others, and it absolutely utterly 100% does *not* mean that you are waiting around all hoity-toitily for others to be thoughtful to *you*. Cripes! Well, that is by the bye.

Back to the point, now: the good news here is that even the toughest woman, the most career-minded feminist, the most secure and together female in all the world, has got needs for such things as companionship and affection. Needs that you can supply! And if you play your cards right, get her into bed too, eventually.

How To

Okay, You Have Managed to Locate a Dumb, Beautiful Woman: Now What?

So now you've got hold of a Patsy, or a reasonably close approximation of one, and you are ready to plan and execute your scheme to get her into bed. You devil, you! Well, here's exactly how you ought to go about it for the maximum chances of success.

Exhibit A. Aristotle Onassis

...was a big cad. He went around on everyone. Not really what you would call an attractive guy, either, not even by the most inclusive and generous standards. And it wasn't

Question: how does this guy (on the left) ...

... wind up with this woman, do you think?

even so much that he was rich, if you ask me. It was more that he described himself as "ruthless," apparently. Meaning, he would do the needful. I suspect he knew how to carry out all the strategies enumerated in this book, and to the *nth* degree.

All sorts of exquisite women fell for him like so many ninepins, including Jacqueline Kennedy and Maria Callas. So I'm bringing Mr. Onassis in here because he was an extremely unprepossessing man from his youth onward, and yet was one of the mid-century's most famously successful lovers.

"I approach every woman as a potential mistress," he once confided to guests on his yacht, as a piano-violin duo serenaded his champagne-sipping guests under the Chinese lanterns. "Beautiful women cannot bear moderation: they need an inexhaustible supply of excess."[1] Here is a man who knew the score.

One way in which Onassis made up for his natural shortcomings was by being perfectly groomed. Sure by being rich, you know. But the guy also knew his threads. Such gorgeous suits such beautiful ties. I've never seen a photograph of Onassis looking other than perfectly turned out. When he was courting Jacqueline Kennedy, he shaved two, even three times a day.[2]

---

[1] Peter Evans, *Nemesis* (New York: HarperCollins, 1996), 85

[2] Ibid.

This is important. Patsy doesn't care whether or not you are goodlooking (she cares whether or not *she* is goodlooking,) but she does care that you are well turned out when you show up at the restaurant or club. So think about the little things, like the quality of your shave. Shave carefully and thoroughly and do not hack your flesh into a bloody pulp. This face, she is thinking, may well be brushing against my own: so not too bristly. And not too much after-shave or cologne, either. It should be lovely cologne, if there is to be cologne. Van Cleef & Arpels which is stunning. Issey Miyake. I have a soft spot for Grey Flannel, too. But just a tiny, tiny bit. Keep in mind that the effect of scent is magnified close up.

Hair. Opinions vary on this subject but one thing is clear: peeking ear and/or nose hair is *totally verboten*. Remove, remove, remove! They have those little whizzy clipper things for the nose ones. Please, this is critical. There are said to be women who like the dread HOB (hair on back,) but I have yet to actually meet one. Certain gay guys, yes. Women, no. Get rid of it. So it hurts to be waxed, indeed it does, my condolences. Eyes on the prize.

Whatever look it is that you plan to be rocking, it must be correct in every particular. Your cuffs must be crisp. Or, your Converse All-Stars must be frayed just so. You're projecting an image to meld into hers, together with everything else you are planning to meld into hers. You're making a fantasy in her mind; you're taking the stage at the center of that fantasy. You can't possibly pay this aspect of the equation too much attention. She'll notice every detail, believe me.

Get Her Alone

If her girlfriends or indeed anyone else is around while you make your case, your chances of getting laid will drop like a rock. The presence of any other sentient being, maybe up to and including a cat, will break the wicked spell you are attempting to weave around Patsy, I'm afraid. Flattery of the type I advise will wilt like a blossom in a blast furnace in the presence of others. Especially if any of those others has got a higher-than-room-temperature IQ. So get her alone.

Alone, where Patsy may drink down your egregious sweet talk unobserved; where she need not experience your utterly unbelievable nonsense in the unforgiving light of reason liable to be produced by her more gimlet-eyed mates. Where she can believe every foolishness you softly whisper into her shell-like ear. Oh, she so wants to believe! You've never felt this way before. She is distracting you. The way she walks drives you mad. Her hair smells so delicious, like flowers, like crushed almonds.

Would she like to dance? Is she getting cold, would she like your jacket? Would she like a nightcap (they have an extraordinary *Eiswein* here, you know.) Is she getting a little tired? Would she like you to take her home?

And so on.

Cough It Up

The single best strategy for getting laid (and that is it) is so idiotically obvious you're really not going to believe it when I tell you. Oh no you won't!! It's so laughably simple. When you think about it the efficacy of this single expedient makes the entire "women are complicated" case collapse like the Tacoma Narrows Bridge. No, we're not so complicated, sad to say.

And in case there are any men of conscience who have slipped past my earlier caveats, I can tell you almost against my better judgment that this advice will work even for non-cads. Yes, even the worthiest, most honorable guy in the world can make use of this advice. If you desire a woman, the best advice I can possibly give you is:

Tell her so.

TELL HER SO.

Say it out loud.

I desire you.
I want you.
I'm on fire for you.
I can barely breathe.
You're making me insane.

I can't stop thinking about you, I can't sleep, I can't eat,
I'm sick with it, I'm going mad. I am dying. I don't know if
I could stand it. I will probably have a
heart attack, have mercy on me. I do
not dare to hope I would survive it.

Phrases like these are not even
like catnip to a susceptible woman. They are more along the lines
of cocaine to a lab rat. This is what
women are programmed to respond
to. It's the blow from the club, and
she's about to be dragged to the cave.
Here is Pavlov's irresistible bell.

You've got to be halfway pre-
sentable and you've got to produce
some flattery with it. You must also
produce, if not absolute conviction,
as least the sly possibility that you

mean exactly what you say. But say it, articulate the desire, demonstrate your despair—and it's a rare woman who will not eventually succumb to the ancient imperative.

Note well: there is a huge difference between asking and demanding, or between confessing a powerful desire for her (which is good) and merely informing her of your wicked intentions (not good.) Remember, too, that this powerful desire isn't just a surge of indiscriminate male libido; you are not just plain consumed by desire, you are consumed by desire for *her*, it is aroused by her and by her only. It is essential, too, to say it in a manner that suggests grave doubts as to the outcome—doubts that only she can allay. Your fate is in the palm of her hand. She should be able to choose, if you see what I mean. Don't be too aggressive with it, or too timid either. That clever, subtle Sun Tzu has got the idea exactly right re: the enemy:

Pretend inferiority and encourage his arrogance.

Hang on her Every Brainless Word

This is important, if you want to get laid. In the case of Patsy, of course, we may well be looking at a formidable challenge. You must truly, deeply listen. As Yoda so wisely says, there is no try. Do, or do not. Get laid, I mean.

It is not enough to look deeply into her eyes as she speaks. You must demonstrate an active interest in what Patsy is saying, grueling though this may be. She is liable to be babbling about the cut-velvet Romeo Gigli skirt she bought on sale at Fred Segal, her total jerk of an ex-boyfriend, or how amazing the sushi is at thus and such a place. Answer her like this:

Oh yeah, really? I love Fred Segal. Who's the designer again?

n.b. do NOT pretend to know anything about fashion that you don't actually know. It is much better to ask a lot of questions, keep her talking.

Oh, Romeo Gigli, Italian, right?

(... and don't ask her any questions that require actual knowledge or expertise, unless you're certain she can answer them.)

I really don't know much about women's designers ... but I love the way you dress.

Touch the fabric of the skirt, if she's wearing it (take your time about that, as if you had hours and hours just for

that.) Ask her to take it out of the bag, if it's in one! Ask
to see it ... tell her shyly:

*I love the way you wear your clothes so much—maybe
you could come shopping with me sometime, because I
could use an expert eye.*

Maybe you think this sounds gay!! Ha ha you are going to
be one lonely guy, if so.

*Some guys don't know how to appreciate a really beau-
tiful, sensitive woman. I think they just feel intimi-
dated in a way, you know? They know they're going to
get dumped, so they feel like they have to get there first.*

Accompany this with a soulful look.

In *no* circumstances sympathize in any way with
the views of Patsy's enemies. Not ever. Never, never. You
may pity them a little bit, because they are lost in the
darkness now forever, banished from the eternal radiance
of Patsy's presence. Too bad for them! Perhaps permit
yourself a sly smile and a remark something like:

*Well in a way, I can't say I'm that sorry ... I'm actually
glad he is such a jerk, or we wouldn't be here right now.*

Oh I love sushi, when can we go? I would love to go there with you sometime soon.

It is all about her, it's the 24/7 Patsy Show, All Patsy All the Time. Not just the tendency or the trajectory of the conversation, but the whole conversation. She is at the wheel all the way. If she asks you a question about yourself (not too likely, this is Patsy we are talking about, after all) answer it directly, and in a way that subtly flatters her taste, her discretion and above all her beauty, every chance you get.

How Long Will This Take?

Impossible to say, I'm afraid. You must be perfectly honest with yourself and be ready to admit defeat, if necessary, but I assure you that with a little patience, victory is assured; if not with this girl, with the next one, or the next. There are certain obstacles that will create difficulties for you from time to time, chief among these being the fact that you may have rivals with a smoother pitch. If so, you must convince Patsy that you alone are the one who loves her most, who needs her most. It really is simply a question of being more extreme, more intense (no, not more abject or out of control. Just more powerfully, dramatically moved by the force of your passion.)

If her eyes begin to glow, if you begin to get a lot of messages on your voicemail, if she begins to turn to you with her troubles, these are all hopeful signs. It's like bodysurfing, you can feel the wave pick you up almost of its own volition; you'll know when the momentum has built up enough that it seems to have a mind of its own. She begins to need you, she wonders when you are going to phone, she starts to take the initiative, her text messages acquire a certain urgency—*omg where were you? I was waiting all day for ur txt!*

The Moment of Truth

Now is the time to pull out all the stops. Your chances of success will rise proportionately with the degree to which you can persuade Patsy that you are in the throes of Ultimate Passion, a violent, irresistible desire that nothing can withstand! You're both about to be overwhelmed ... this thing is bigger than both of you. The key here is to show that you have been brought to the brink of annihilation by her beauty and desirability. She's made you lose sight of everything you ever cared about, leaving only her ... her alone. In case you are super clueless and need pointers on how to convey Ultimate Passion, you might check out the final scenes of *The Return of the King*, in which Frodo Baggins has been slowly driven mad by his desire for the One

Ring. You can practically quote these last lines, lightly edited for the occasion. Of course if it turns out Patsy is a big dork and loves Tolkien (highly, *highly* unlikely,) you are maybe courting a little trouble.

> *Sam: Do you remember the Shire, Mr. Frodo? It'll be spring soon. And the orchards will be in blossom. And the birds will be nesting in the hazel thicket. And they'll be sowing the summer barley in the lower fields... and eating the first of the strawberries with cream. Do you remember the taste of strawberries?*

> *Frodo: No, Sam. I can't recall the taste of food... nor the sound of water... nor the touch of grass. I'm... naked in the dark, with nothing, no veil... between me... and the wheel of fire! I can see him... with my waking eyes!*

(Practice in the mirror, if necessary.)

When you first kiss her, make a great show of being moved almost to tears. You've never felt anything like it. Whisper this stuff to her, very soft and low. You're so moved, it's so incredible ... you can't bear it.

Half an hour or so of this pleasant bushwah, and she will be begging you to take her home.

But What if It's All True?

Oh, indeed?—so much the better. (But wait, are you telling me that you actually *are* a gentleman, and not just acting like one? That you have found a woman who has brought you to your knees with molten, incandescent passion, whose conversation really does fascinate you, whose company you crave, night and day?? You weren't just acting—really?! You're kidding! If you really do feel that you are about to expire from Ultimate Passion, I can almost guarantee that everything is going to go pretty swimmingly for quite a while. For the duration, even, maybe.)

If you're anything like my old friend Templeton, of course, Ultimate Passion tends to last for a matter of days ... maybe weeks. At that point you've got a new set of problems, one I can't help you with. I only said I would tell you more or less how to get there, not how to get back out again.

This Templeton is the kind of man who loves all women. He really does. He is what is called The Romantic Type. He's a good-looking rogue, too, brilliant, entertaining, lovely manners, almost courtly, very well-spoken, well-dressed. When I first met him, we were with a gang of loosely-connected old friends who all found themselves in New York one weekend. It was dinner with these friends, drinks with those, so we kept running into one another. Hilariously, Templeton was laying his snares for at least two of us females, to my knowledge, this same weekend. He phoned me on my cell, quite late.

Templeton.	Where are you? I'm at a bar across the street.
Me.	Across the street from where?
Templeton.	From your hotel. It's no fun being in this town without your woman.
Me.	Good lord.
Templeton.	How soon can you be down here?
Me.	I can't go out now!?! Are you nuts? It's after midnight.
Templeton.	Come on. They make a damn fine martini. Just like you like 'em.

When this did not work, I expect he proceeded to mow down the list until he struck gold somehow. Here's another secret: even though I knew that I was being played like a violin, and that I was just one on a list (not even no. 1, I'm sure!) I just couldn't find it in me to be mad at Templeton. He was so transparent that his machinations seemed harmless. It didn't hurt either that he was so charming, so good-looking. There is often so very little risk to the Templetons of this world in this approach, it isn't even funny. Because we women really do love to be courted.

We love to be loved.

Even, truth to tell, just-kidding love, like Templeton's. But what would happen is that some injudicious female would respond to him in that same just-kidding way, and each joke led to another, less-kidding one, and pretty soon all hell had broken loose, with children and spouses flying in every direction.

Sadly, Templeton was on his fifth marriage by the time we lost touch. He was burning out on the romance thing, I think. He looked exhausted in that way those books on Eastern medicine describe, with the sunken red-rimmed eyes and whatnot from extreme sensuality and baths and various other forms of excess. The Walter Pater approach will do that to you. He wrote:

> *To burn always with this hard, gem-like flame,*
> *to maintain this ecstasy, is success in life.*

Now, listen to me! That is crazy talk. Yes, I am telling you how to get laid, but the sad fact is that nobody can maintain this ecstasy for so very long as all that, because the terminals just start to fry. So please, now that I am providing you with all the secrets you need, I hope you will consider taking it easy on the serial seduction thing, just for the sake of your own sanity.

THE EXPENSE

This is in the same class with Penis Size, another foolish red herring that can only distract you from your objective. Do I need to remind you of all the "unsuitable men" girls have fallen for throughout recorded history? Do girls go falling in love with some clown because he is spending money on them?! No, they do not. They fall in love (etc.) with some clown who has paid court to them.

No matter what your means, it will be child's play for you to attend to many, many of the preferences of whatever female it is you mean to take to bed, and satisfy those, and it will not cost a lot. In the matter of gifts and little attentions, the things she likes to eat and drink, her favorite flowers and music—few of these will be expensive (unless she is so utterly vapid that I really cannot help but question your taste, and will advise you to move on to a higher-quality specimen.) The gift chosen with attention and care is worth a million times more to almost any woman, up to and including a Patsy, than an ostentatious one with no emotional provenance. A gift that unmistakably indicates Ultimate Passion—a poem or song you wrote for her, a mix CD that you made of her favorite music, things you've shared together, some token of a private joke, a photograph of something shared and personal—such things are the most valuable gifts to women (all women!) and their cost is trivial.

via flickr photographer telethon, creative commons

So I don't want to hear a lot of excuses about how you are not getting laid because all women are spoiled brats, an expensive hobby, and you can't afford them. That is a sour-grapes argument, as specious as it is unbecoming.

It's true that there really is such a thing as the so-called "gold-digger" who is out to squeeze guys for what she can get. But they are extremely rare and unless you really are positively rolling in it, you probably won't even run across one.

Please do not mistake the woman who in time displays some interest in your professional circumstances with the one who is looking to bleed you dry. An ordinary woman will be evincing curiosity on this point mainly in order to make sure you're together enough, not just professionally but as an adult, that you won't become a liability to her. Not just with regard to money, you know, but because professional stability is a good indicator of stability in general, she'll assume that if you're halfway okay professionally, you won't be falling apart all over the place in other areas. Believe it or not, there are a lot of messed-up, troubled guys out there who sponge off of women, too, emotionally, financially, every which way.

What a downer! Enough about all that dismal stuff. We were talking about wooing, comma, negligible expenses attendant thereupon.

Not just the principal but the only thing really required of you is to adore this girl. But given that you want to get her in bed without delay, there are a lot of things that even the man of limited means can do to turn up the passion without huge expenditures. This is all about the trouble you took, and are taking, on her behalf. If you cook, you must cook for her; if a musician, you will play for her, compose for her; if an artist, you will present her with a drawing of herself. If you can manage to persuade her that no other woman could ever make you go to such lengths, she will almost certainly respond. You're showing her that you are looking forward to sharing her company with every little move you make, so take advantage. Learn all about her and you will get all the cues you need as to how to make her feel flattered, valued, pursued.

I was once courted by a very beautiful young man who had literally gone to the trouble of *making furniture* in anticipation of my arrival in New York. He was poor as a churchmouse, but I couldn't have felt more loved or valued if he had been the Prince of Wales. Do you see what I am getting at, here? Again, it's not the expense, it's the *attention*. It's the fact that you did something delightful, something difficult or challenging for her, willingly; that you are offering her something of yourself, without the slightest hope of anything in return, just as a tribute to her desirability, out of admiration and esteem. Now she is feeling that you're so splendid and so wonderful, you see? Shouldn't she give back, give you all the things you'd like from her, in return?

Why yes, of course she should.

YOUR VIRILITY
IN DANGER (NOT.)

I have had the same email address for over ten years, and it has been spidered all over the place, one way and another. The upshot being that I get quite a lot of spam, a huge proportion of which is spam from sadly mistaken persons who assume that I am a man who needs help with his sex life [*sic* throughout, naturally.]

Do you want enalarge yours p3n1s up to 4 inches

lift your sweet night adventures assistance worthwhiled medicines.

Make her moann in pleasure every single time!

You can be rock hard all day long. [ow]

Be a stallion in bed

Enlarging your device means enlarging your manliness overall.

Make your lady's peaks of pleasure your usual achievement!
Your virility will never be destroyed as long as you remain with us.
Never finish fast in bed

and my favorite,

heave your darling bed experience with relef of precious drugs.

The most perplexing thing about all of this is that any-body could find any of the above appeals the slightest bit compelling. The theme of male "performance" appears directly linked to that great mysterious subject of Penis Size. Should men really be so concerned about Penis Size??

You have heard this before, but I find I have to say it again.

No!

No, no no no no. The man in search of relef has in general got nothing to worry about regarding the size of his device. What he needs to be worrying about is identifying his quarry, and then paying it truckloads of attention. Maybe once in a very great while there is such a thing as a man who is under-endowed but believe me, if he can make with the truckloads of attention, even the al-legedly underendowed man has got *nothing to worry about*. Because I cannot say this often enough: what a woman wants from you is NOT a huge penis, it is attention. It is Ultimate Passion.

It can only hinder you to be worrying about such irrelevancies, which proceed from the fact that men persist in assuming that women are the same as themselves, but with different equipment. They assume that since men like naked pictures of women, women like naked pictures of men, etc. I hope you are starting to understand how very wrong about all that you've been.

While I am on the subject, though: what is the deal with you guys all worrying about your virility being destroyed? How would that even happen? It sounds weirdly like those guys who become convinced that their penises have been or are about to be stolen; q.v. Wikipedia under "penis panic" or "genital retraction syndrome," I am not kidding. According to them, "Penis panics in southeast Asia have become known under the term 'Koro'" (which "means 'head of the turtle' in Malay," evidently.)

Y'all have got the wrong end of the device, yet again. You must learn to stop worrying about "failing to perform." Women never, ever complain about about men not satisfying them because of their size, or really for any other reason. I was going to say, "sane women," or "intelligent women," and then I realized no, just never, this never happens. Just get that idea clean out of your head. Understand that even if a woman doesn't achieve orgasm, she will most assuredly blame not you, but herself.

Have a look at the sex guides for women out there. They are telling women how to achieve multiple orgasms, and making them feel rather guilty if they aren't ready to have at least five or six at one go. There are no sex guides called "How to Find a Guy with the Biggest Dick Imaginable, Really Scary Big, in Order to Achieve Satisfaction," or anything of this nature. Books on sexual technique written for women are always about relaxing, having a glass of wine, getting in touch with your sensations and all that hokum so that you can lie back and have a zillion orgasms. *Nobody is blaming, or has ever blamed, or will ever blame, your penis size.* Nobody that I ever met, or read about or even heard of, anyway. Because: women are every bit as paranoid as you are about "performance."

Check out *Cosmopolitan* sometime. Do you think there has ever been an article in *Cosmo* entitled, "My No-Good Man's Penis is Only Four Inches Long, So I Can't Have an Orgasm. Bah!" No. It's all "Six Easy Ways to Make Him Scream with Ecstasy" and "How to Give the Perfect Blowjob."

Now, you have heard over and over again, I am sure, that many if not most women require an emotional connection in order to consummate the act of love. So how do you expect to address all that merely by having an extra-large penis? Please, re-read the title of this book and *think like a woman* for a minute. Women may appreciate a beautiful guy with no shirt on but it is in a purely aesthetic, detached way, the way you might admire a painting or a garden or a pretty child. In women, the visual imagination is not connected to their erogenous zones, the way it is with men. Sexual feeling for women is cerebral, not physical, in its origin.

Orgasm for women is not the same as for men, either ("almost entirely a matter of friction," as my husband has alarmingly disclosed.) Foolish, nonsensical advice columns written by men are full of idiotic advice about locating the clitoris, the g-spot, all explained in bogus clinical terms, nerve endings, blood flow and so on, and are really, really absurd and counterproductive for you.

Her erogenous zones will sort themselves out just beautifully if only you say how bewitching she looks, if only you whisper how you desire her, how you must have her right now, how you can't believe this moment is finally happening, etc. *ad infinitum.*

The one thing the manuals are correct in saying is that you need to take your time in the bedroom. Younger guys will necessarily have trouble with this, but it is an absolute must. Hold off if necessary by thinking of baseball scores, Margaret Thatcher, or the magical incantation devised by a friend of my husband's in his younger days: "dead fish Grandma dead fish Grandma." It is perfectly fine to reboot, of course, just yeah, make sure you take enough time for her. That's the one "performance" issue that really does count.

The general tenor of these spams I get all the time doesn't seem to be in the least concerned with the desire for female companionship, but is instead one of nervousness with regard to various questions of virility. There are certainly better ways of locating and enjoying female companionship than worrying about things like this. There are lots and lots of them.

I used to know this really handsome English guy who had gotten the picture with such clarity. He told me that he had taken pains to become a good dancer from his earliest days, because he'd realized that most guys do not like to dance, but girls love it. So he could ask girls to dance, and be relatively certain of a warm reception. This guy is so amusing and so gorgeous that he could probably have just sat still and a lot of girls would have just swarmed all over him anyway, but there you go. I am certain that he never lacked for willing company.

There is no spam, you will observe, advising men to ask women to dance, which would be a far more effective means of ensuring a satisfying sex life for men. And women, come to that. (Hey, though ... maybe someone could come up with a jOn tRav01t4 Disko!!!%!% Pill 4 U! Spam marketers, take heed.)

A Note to Guys who Think They Ought to be Taking Those Penis Enlargement Pills.

If you think that the sight of a guy with a great big penis is going to drive every woman crazy with lust despite herself, your expectations are 100% wrong. You understand this now, right?

Since we are on the subject, I may as well add right now that there really is such a thing as too big. Even if these penis enlargement pills worked—which *I just bet they don't* and plus, what if there is harmful stuff in there?—I mean, "an extra four inches!" and so on, let me just tell you. That would be a disaster in almost every respect. Come on! Four extra inches is a hell of a lot, as regards penis size. What women want is attention! They do NOT want you to suddenly appear flaunting some twelve-inch monster that they wouldn't even begin to be able to accommodate. That would strike not lust but *terror* into their hearts. What they would be thinking of is not sweet love, so much as potential disembowelment.

THE L-WORD

There is a very powerful magic word that can set women (and especially Patsies) on fire. Almost by itself, this magic word is liable to bring Patsy's defenses crashing down, flimsy or firm as those may be. For some incomprehensible reason, however, men do not care to say this word.

So simple! Just one little syllable, consisting of one (1) voiced lateral approximant, one (1) back mid vowel, and one (1) voiced labial fricative. That's it! I highly recommend that you practice repeating this very simple word until it positively trips off the tongue. I am certain that you can do this! Go on, try it now. Say it a few times, just to grease the wheels a bit. You'll be going on to use this word in the phrase:

I love you [áj ləv jú]

Please think about this for a moment. There are over four thousand hits on the exact phrase "men don't say I love you" on Google right now. Why on earth not, you fools!?

Now think, man. Pull your socks together. You *told* me that what you want is sex. Look over the crazy reasoning above and please, explain to me how a clever, manipulative creature like you could possibly get in the slightest bit of trouble merely by saying three little words that can be taken back, with a wily display of tears if you are capable of summoning them up, at any time. Or you may prefer to go on to explain what a *lot* of women you are in love with, if you decide you want some distance between yourself and your no-longer-so-fascinating inamorata. If you have not been lying to me, and what you want is to get in some woman's pants, this phrase is like a supernatural charm for getting your wicked way. Whyever wouldn't you avail yourself of this miraculous tool?

After thinking it over, I have come up with a number of reasons why you might not like to say the L-word, as follows: 1) you have a deep-seated reluctance to lie, and you know that you don't, in fact, love Patsy; 2) you fear that you are making more of a commitment than you are yet ready to make; 3) you fear she will reject you, pat you on the head, say, "I just want to be friends" or something like this; 4) the vulnerability scares you; 5) seems sissy; 6) you imagine that you'll lessen the validity of something by speaking it, in some kind of voodoo or WASP manner.

Let's go through your putative objections one by one.

1. **Honesty.** You straight-up don't love Patsy, you just want to sleep with her. This is assuming first off that you have a concept of love that is something above, or entirely distinct from, your nefarious intentions for this girl. It's like, you're saving yourself for something better, an as-yet-unknown ideal. Does this make any sense at all? No. If you have a more elevated concept of the Real Thing, something still more desirable, why not go forth and try to satisfy that?! You're only wasting time, really, and life is short. You might get hit by a bus at any moment.

Let's assume, alternatively, that what you mean is that you're not interested in the Real Thing right *now*, but are just practicing at love; then why not enter into the spirit of romance and adventure you are feeling now, and say it? Why not give yourself license to feel like a great lover, and say it? Why not enjoy the moment, and say it? Don't you feel it just right now, just this minute? Surely you can manage to say it, then.

2. **Commitment.** Saying the L-word does not commit you to anything at all. In fact, the sum of your intentions for Patsy, which is to get her to go to bed with you with no strings attached, practically demands dissimulation on this point. That is to say, she pretty much *needs* to think that you're feeling more seriously about her than you really are. To put this as baldly as possible: success for you quite possibly relies, to some extent, on guile. Therefore, your argument collapses. You're already deceiving her, admit it; you needn't deceive yourself. Use the tools!

Telling her that you love her does not mean that you have to let her move into your apartment, or agree to father her child, not today. All it means, for today, is that you have been carried away by your desire. Any Patsy worthy of the name can be quite easily distracted from thorny questions of marriage or shacking up by an appeal to Ultimate Passion. You've been driven crazy, remember, by her desirability. Just keep coming back to that, and Bob's your uncle.

If she insists on some kind of commitment-inter-rogation you'll tell her, yes, I love you, but I'm just not *ready* yet to give you all you deserve, I'm "not where I want to be in my life," etc. etc. Nothing could be simpler.

3. **Fear of Rejection.** You aren't going to say it until you know for certain that she's ready to hear it. You'll know

exactly when. You've been describing to her for days or weeks how beautiful she is, how desirable. You've magically created this wonderful fantasy world for the two of you to inhabit ... you'll certainly know in advance when you've already got her coming back to hear more about Ultimate Passion. You'll know, believe me. And it's going to be a really climactic moment, if you'll pardon the phrase. You'll say it—no you'll *confess*, in great pain, great torment—you'll practically have a nervous breakdown! And a side order of tears, too, if you can manage it. My god, you can't bear it. Will she have mercy on you?

Oh, you'll be pouring it on like a regular Rudolph Valentino. At that point it will be a matter of days, if not hours or minutes, until your goal is achieved.

4. **Vulnerability.** See (2) and (3) above. You're not vulnerable, because you are not committed. Not *really* committed, that is; it's just for this moment, or just for show. You get carried away with yourself, if you see what I mean. You'll see. If you're like every other womanizer in this world, you'll get into it so much that you'll very easily be able to discuss raw sexual feeling in the language of real passion, and actually be swept away by the drama, the moment, and come to believe it all yourself.

Another secret: women very fervently believe that it is better to have loved and lost, etc. Much, much much better. A grown woman without a string of heartbreaks be-hind her is reckoned rather a poor specimen (UK "saddo") among women, particularly among the Romantic Type. Consequently, even though it is not going to "work out," as the phrase is, if you play your cards right by continuing to refer nostalgically to your glorious past with Patsy—by letting go gracefully, and without rancor or cruelty—there is no reason to suppose there will be any lasting harm on either side. On the contrary, a passionate love affair is self-evidently a success just by virtue of having happened at all, leaving only a trail of beautiful bittersweet memo-ries in its wake and, with any luck, no lasting sadness.

You needn't fear rejection, either, because you know she is already taking the bait, and so she will most certainly swallow all your delicious lies down like a torrent of nectar.

5. **Sissy.** Certainly not! What you're putting across is that you are a powerful man brought low by the uncontrollable force of his desire. Like Humphrey Bogart's head collaps-ing onto his arms at the table at Rick's, after Ingrid Berg-man has taken herself off. It's not embarrassing soppiness, and there's nothing sissy about it. Quite the reverse.

Men are very protective of their *amour-propre*, it is true. They dislike wearing silly hats, singing in public and so on. Anything that doesn't jibe with the strong and silent, they think, must be an unmanly thing. As in, if you cease to be silent, you cease to be manly. You fear to look foolish, because that would be terribly un-manly and un-virile. Please note however that among women, a man's willingness to display emotion is reckoned precisely the opposite way; the bold man is the one who has courage enough to say exactly what is on his mind, to take the rare risk of speaking. The habitual repression and silence of his fellows is nothing but a boon to the calculating man. Consider the power you might get from speaking (enormous) as against the risk of sissiness, which is pretty much nil so far as women are concerned.

For proof of this, look how popular all these professional musicians are with women. Girls do not fall all over themselves on behalf of muscle-bound bricklayers, but rather, on behalf of wet, weedy singers who look like they couldn't bench press five pounds. Singing itself is not a particularly manly pursuit, you will agree. And yet, famous musicians are irresistible to beautiful girls; they're probably the most sought-after males in the whole of our great nation. These guys are generally the most accomplished adepts in the art of seduction, too, and in no need of reading this book; 'twas ever thus. Donovan, for example, was forever bleating to some girl about how he wanted to get inside the warm hold of her, ah. *"Mind,"* apparently. Sinatra, whose foolish heart was so touched by The Way She Looked Tonight, was a categorical Don Juan. Tommy Lee is not on the face of it a very prepossessing specimen, either, and yet he too manages to convey a strangely attractive vulnerability; the perfect front for that ardent, if scrawny and much-tattooed, Casanova.

Please note that all these guys are basically doing is telling the women they want, or singing to them, rather, the L-word.

Even the Owl knew exactly how to go about this, way back in 1871. As you will recall:

> *The Owl and the Pussy-cat went to sea*
> *In a beautiful pea-green boat,*
> *They took some honey, and plenty of money,*
> *Wrapped up in a five-pound note.*
> *The Owl looked up to the stars above,*
> *And sang to a small guitar,*
> *'O lovely Pussy! O Pussy my love,*
> *What a beautiful Pussy you are,*
> *You are,*
> *You are!*
> *What a beautiful Pussy you are!'*

Now, observe how the Pussy-cat falls like a ton of oh-so-predictable bricks *in the very next line*:

Pussy said to the Owl, 'You elegant fowl!
How charmingly sweet you sing!
O let us be married! too long we have tarried:
But what shall we do for a ring?'

As in, *practically the very moment the guitar is produced.*

6. The Unspoken. That is all very well, but what we are discussing here is your chances of getting this girl in bed. You can't be too solipsistic about this, hoping she will be sensitive enough to enter into your feelings and divine them all, for that will certainly result in unnecessary delay. Unless you are very serious indeed and willing to wait for eons, there is no point in protecting passion's tenderness. Lay it all out before her instead; speak it; and maybe even

see how love can in fact blossom more richly, too, where it is spoken and returned.

Men have often told me that they simply don't know what to say to women about love. They're not sure when they are in love; perhaps they are just randy; they are baffled, not knowing what their feelings are. They know that they are in lust—there is no mistaking that—but love? Should a man think himself a heel, or a fool, if he is in danger of confusing one thing with the other?

On the other hand, perhaps he knows very clearly that he is not in love, but that is not at all the point, for he knows he is in lust, and that is a highly distracting state. It is a great disadvantage to men that lust can come down on them like an avalanche, giving no warning and over-whelming all their senses quite separately from anything they may actually be able to reason out about themselves, about women, or about the state of their own notions of love and companionship.

I suspect that a great number of you never even get anywhere *near* testing out your own real convictions be-cause in actual practice, you are instantly waylaid by your uncontrollable libido, which takes charge of your whole lives and hurls you blind into a roaring cascade of near-madness; thereby ensuring that if there is any cogitation to be done, it will only take place long after the havoc has already been wrought. You might think that over a bit sometime, with a view to putting the horse before the cart, for a change.

But for the moment, you have a goal in mind. So say the L-word, say it, say it say it. Say it over and over again.

THE HANDSOME PRINCE: OR, ULTIMATE PASSION, JR., A GUIDE FOR SERIOUS STUDENTS OF THE INTERIOR WORKINGS OF THE HEARTS AND MINDS OF WOMEN

The irresistible allure of passion starts early for women—perhaps at about age two, when the Handsome Prince first enters the picture-book. Long before they have the faintest clue what such things really mean or might entail, little girls are introduced to that mythical beast, the Handsome Prince, to the beauty and charm of Princesses, and to the associated arts of love; and these are imprinted on their wee consciousnesses, together and severally, forever and ever. In order for you to produce a credible demonstration of Ultimate Passion, it will help you to understand these phenomena very clearly (and no, I am not going to ask you to wear tights. Though let's face it, if you really thought that tights would get you laid, I bet you would wriggle into a pair right now.)

Ask most any little girl, age four or so, what she would like to be for Halloween, and she will tell you: a

Illustration from My Book House, 1920

Princess. She has a Princess bedroom, with Princess wallpaper and Princess dolls and movies, and probably at least one tiara or crown. Her highest praise for any article of wearing apparel is that it is "a Princess one." Already she has come to see herself as a Princess; her grandfather calls her, "Princess"; when she appears in public decked out in unusually delicious finery for some wedding or party, all will gratifyingly exclaim: "Sweetie! You look just like a Princess!"

These girlish fantasies aren't harmful, in and of themselves. They are fun!—I will say at once, I find even those rather skanky Bratz dolls quite delightful. I don't know why! They have cute boots and accessories. Anyway, we introduce children male and female to the world's unpleasant realities, the death-and-taxes tough stuff, just a little at a time, as they become ready to take on each new bit of ghastliness. So we don't really tell girls about the Princess thing being kind of fictitious for quite some time. In the same way, grown men are well past the idea that they are going to grow up to be James Bond, yet still they can have fun watching James Bond, even though they are grownups and they no longer believe that this is the way the world works at all, and that is absolutely A. O-K, right? Yes. So eventually many women, too, come to put away such childish things as fairy-tales and Bratz dolls, and realize, not with dismay but with passionate conviction and determination, that they must work to create their own heaven on earth and all of that, while still being able to enjoy a fairy tale once in a while.

Nevertheless, a lot of these Princess stories are explicitly telling little girls that they haven't got any agency for themselves, and they don't need to develop any, either. What they need to be doing is hanging around, growing hair, or maybe weaving a tapestry, for years and years, and waiting. Someone else is going to be coming along one day to put an end to all their little troubles. That old, old story. Just today, in this restaurant at lunch, they were playing an old standard expressing exactly this same sentiment ("Someone to Watch Over Me," in which the singer, a grown woman, describes herself as "a little lamb who's lost in a wood" without her as-yet-unknown protector. Who, presumably, is a Prince, and not a border collie.)

Even the most up-to-date retellings of these old stories bump up against the same great big insurmountable difficulty: the fact that the hero must be the powerful one, the savior. He must still save the princess, no matter what. We have not moved one millimeter past this thorny problem, which features in *Sex and the City* as surely as it does in Cinderella. No matter how independent and together a heroine is portrayed to be, the hero still has to save her, and make all her dreams come true (cf. *Star Wars, Raiders of the Lost Ark* and even *Pride and Prejudice.*)

This is maybe not the greatest fantasyland to have built for girls big or small, entertaining though it may be. It would take a far longer book than ours (to say nothing of a way smarter author) to explain how it all came about. But come about it did; and what is more, it would take a meaner woman than myself to confiscate any little girl's tiara. There is something very touching about little girls, gazing at themselves in the mirror in their gauzy wings and glittering little crowns. The tenderness and sweetness of a girl admiring her first playground champion—that doughty little hero who would not permit her hair to be pulled, nor her toy filched—that is a lovely thing. I love to see anyone enjoying a fantasy, being absorbed in the spirit of play, and that is the way girls play. Maybe there is even something more to it, something to do with how we're made, the real differences between men and women that stubbornly defy alteration—I don't presume to say.

What we are concentrating on here is how to use this state of affairs to your advantage, in order to get some girl or other into bed.

So: what did our tiny little Patsy know about Princesses? That they are very pretty, that they have beautiful clothes and jewels (with *real* diamonds, not plastic,) and most of all, that Princesses are wonderfully happy forever and ever, once the Prince rescues them and takes them to the castle. The Prince is very lovely and kind, indeed he looks and behaves quite a bit like their kindergarten teacher (see illustration *supra*, minus the chain mail) except that he loves and cares for only one special Princess whom he will call his own, and there will be a lot of finery all round, and as for the lucky Princess's horrible, icky enemies and rivals, they will be utterly blasted and destroyed.

I asked my husband, did you ever see yourself, when you were a little boy, as a Handsome Prince? No indeed, he said. Those were girls' stories. Besides, he said, the prince is just a MacGuffin.

This is hilariously true! The Prince hardly matters a bit, except insofar as he must admire and save the Princess; he's amazingly characterless, whether we examine his bizarre behavior in the Disney version of *Sleeping Beauty* or in the oldest Cinderella story, it's utterly beside the point; the story is ever and always All About Her. Is this starting to sound familiar? It should!

The fact is that some girls never do move past this phase, and their name is Patsy. Therefore, in order to get what you need from a vulnerable creature of this kind:

You are the Handsome Prince.

Make every effort to see yourself this way, in relation to her. If you can't produce the royal blood, a horse, or a castle, that is no big deal. You just need to appear as her admirer and champion in all things, gentle, winning, capable, and ready to launch into a fruity-sounding duet at the drop of a hat. Remember, from the moment you clapped eyes on this girl, your every mooning thought has been of her.

You don't like that idea, eh? Sounds corny and weird! Okay then, lonely guy.

You think it's committing you to a lifetime of galloping around on a horse?! No! Note well that all these stories do is win the day. "Happily ever after" is always left curiously undefined. These are *courtship* stories, not marriage stories. You are free to define "happily ever after" as lasting for a matter of weeks or even days, if you like. It is all a *folie à deux,* a fantasy built for two.

Really, you could do far worse than watch a few Disney films (say, *Sleeping Beauty, Cinderella* and maybe *The Little Mermaid*) in order to pick up a few hints. (Not *Beauty and the Beast*, though! That one is an outlier, way too complex, and too advanced, to illustrate this point.)

Maybe you think this early imprinting is not such a big deal, that adult women aren't affected by it. *Au contraire, mon frère!* It never really goes away, not entirely. It only gets worse and worse, in many cases. By the time a girl gets to be twelve or thirteen, the desire is liable to have swollen into an almost excruciating pain. She is thinking hey, I am suffering, so where is my Prince?

For evidence of this, one need look no farther than

the Teen Idol. You've probably noticed that there is a strong preference among young girls for very bland, effeminate teenage boys—singers usually, sometimes actors—fantasy figures closely and creepily resembling themselves, from Fabian to Donny Osmond, Davy Jones and David Cassidy right through to Hanson and the Jonas Brothers and, I daresay, Michael Cera. These proto-sex-objects are utterly unthreatening and gentle and just plain lovely, barely male at all, smooth, hairless, and they would all fit with ease into the jeans of their slenderest, most flat-chested admirers. (Aside: I am compelled to add here that the Teen Idol is a temporary fixation. Grown women who are no longer scared of men, and who love them—who prefer to take their masculinity straight up, as it were, rather than drowned in syrup and cherries—find themselves much more attracted to the real thing, so please, not to worry about having developed the secondary sexual characteristics. Those are very charming to grown women, just not to adolescent ones—but have your back waxed! Seriously.)

Weirdly, the sight of these effeminate boys can make adolescent girls scream, swoon, weep and faint. What is up with that? They are virgins! They have no pubic hair, even. They literally don't even know exactly what it is they are pining for, yet they are shrieking for all the world like somebody is after them with a chainsaw.

photo by Matt Dinerstein

ECSTASY AND DESPAIR
OF ADOLESCENT GIRLS
IN THE PRESENCE
OF IMPROBABLY-NAMED TEEN IDOL
CORBIN BLEU

Here is why: they are wild with longing for the very thing they were taught to long for when they were two. They've been waiting forever and their hair has grown clear down to the ground from that lonely tower, and where is their Prince, they would like to know? Someday their prince would come, they were told.

So imagine all this happening back in 1964, when a maiden first caught sight of the downy, fey and poetical young Paul McCartney. Really, the only thing missing was the horse. Here he was, handsome as hell, "the gentleman with the long hair" and the anime eyes, and he loved her, yeah, yeah yeah! Far from being grossed out or even just nonplussed by girls, like all the grubby adolescent boys of her own acquaintance, this gentle, effeminate Prince was *already singing*, even—and you guessed it, about Love, yeah, yeah, yeah wooooo.

They wanted him so badly they were weeping, and screaming, and fainting in their millions.

Or take the crazily popular teen novel (and recently, film,) *Twilight*. The enormous appeal of this unbelievably terrible novel is a mystery to most literature fans, but I read it and I can tell you that its appeal is 100% about sex, despite the fact that it depicts no sex, and that it was written by a Mormon housewife. As awful as this book is from a purely literary standpoint, there is not the least doubt that it's very sexy. To twelve-year-old girls. It's sex for virgins, the safest sex there is, with the restraint turned up to Eleven and tons and tons of longing, intimacy and mad, barely controllable desire, also turned up to Eleven.

I mean you have to wonder, what the heck, you go on Facebook and practically every teenage girl has got little buttons and things all over that say Mrs. Edward Cullen (he is the teen vampire hero, though he is really 90 or something, ew.) My daughter's best friend and millions like her were ready to crawl to the bookstore on their hands and knees over broken glass to get hold of each book in the series, as it came out.

Vampire vealcake Robert Pattinson, via Wikimedia Commons

The first one, *Twilight*, consists of hundreds and hundreds of pages of exceedingly tame foreplay that succeed in communicating the (neverending) dawning of lust. There's enough lightly sexualized blue-ballin' foreplay in that book to choke Barbara Cartland. Most importantly, the heroine is just an ordinary girl who attracts an utterly extraordinary (gorgeous immortal vampire) boy, so the book creates a fantasy world wherein the most ordinary girl can imagine that sort of earth-shattering love for herself. Here's this dreamboat with all sorts of self-control, you know, who asks only to be allowed to worship and protect her. He does nothing but restrain his Ultimate Passion, Jr., night and day. He comes to her bedroom every night and watches her *sleep*, seriously, protects her from every possible harm, etc. He's the most awesome, unusual, immortal, perfect, stone-cold undead white marble vampire boyfriend evah. And she spends chapter after chapter trying to get him to get to second base.

That's right SHE is constantly trying to get HIM to go a little farther, but he WON'T.

Don't laugh, man. Vampire boy was onto something.

A LITTLE STRANGE

This is a term men use to refer to casual sex outside a relationship. It frequently appears, alas, in the would-be jaunty construction, "get me some strange." On urbandictionary.com some guy describes a bar as, "crawling with strange." Scary, eh? Women really do not understand what they are up against, here. With some guys this thing is so pronounced that they appear to be reckoning women up as a totally undifferentiated commodity. A giant squelching mass of potential novelty, as it were.

I mention this in order to point out the blinding difference between men's attitudes and those of women regarding the question of a new partner. Often and often, men make the mistake of assuming that women are constituted like themselves regarding *anything* related to the act of love. Here is an error that will positively guarantee failure on so many fronts that it is really worth going into some detail, in order to ensure you avoid it.

While women's feelings regarding the notion of "a little strange" tend to hover in the meh-to-terrified range, the idea is a hugely popular one with males throughout the animal kingdom. The "Coolidge Effect" has even been *scientifically proven* to be far less pronounced in females than in males (specifically, in female hamsters.)

Calvin Coolidge, via Wikimedia Commons

For those who are unfamiliar with this phrase: our 30th President, "Silent Cal," may have been total rubbish as a President, but he was a great wag, whether or not you care to include this probably apocryphal story. Here's an excerpt from the relevant Wikipedia entry:

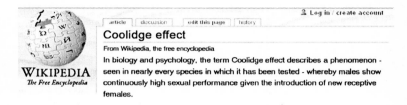

Origin of the term

The term comes from an old joke, according to which President Calvin Coolidge and his wife allegedly visited a poultry farm. During the tour, Mrs. Coolidge inquired of the farmer how his farm managed to produce so many fertile eggs with such a small number of roosters. The farmer proudly explained that his roosters performed their duty dozens of times each day.

"Perhaps you could point that out to Mr. Coolidge," pointedly replied the First Lady.

The President, overhearing the remark, asked the farmer, "Does each rooster service the same hen each time?"

"No," replied the farmer, "there are many hens for each rooster."

"Perhaps you could point that out to Mrs. Coolidge," replied the President.

Empirical evidence

The original experiments with rats followed this protocol: A male rat would be placed into an enclosed large box with four or five female rats in estrus. He would immediately begin mating with all of the female rats repeatedly until eventually exhausted. Although the females would continue nudging and licking him to continue, he would not respond. However, if a novel female were introduced to the box, he would become alert and find the ability to mate once again with the new female. This phenomenon is not limited to *Rattus norvegicus*. It is attributed to an increase in dopamine levels and its subsequent effect upon the limbic system.

While the Coolidge effect is usually seen demonstrated by males – that is, males displaying renewed excitement with a novel female – Lester and Gorzalka developed a model to determine whether or not the Coolidge effect also occurs in females. Their experiment, which used hamsters instead of rats, found that it does occur in lesser degrees in females.

We can take it as read that men and women (and hamsters, if they are on the ball) know instinctively that males are far more susceptible to novelty than are females.

flickr photograph courtesy of cdrussorusso, creative commons

So, you come here often?

For women, A Little Strange is apt to loom with the ominous possibility of being A Lot Strange.

Novelty itself, then, is of very great value, to most men. For men particularly constituted in this way, women are an asset whose depreciation accelerates at an ever-increasing rate—and very fast to start with, because a woman's novelty-value disappears almost instantly, like a new car you've just driven off the lot. My ex confirms that for a lot of men, there is a kind of lizard-brain response to the mere idea of A New One, together with a corresponding urge to keep pressing that button, over and over. I've always wondered about that, though. We are asked to believe that no man would ever choose a companion for life, except that he was hoodwinked into it by some female; for if he had his druthers, it would be hen after hen after hen after hen. It seems to me however that nobody ever asked the original rooster how *he* felt about what really must be the increasing drudgery of constant novelty-copulation. Wouldn't novelty itself lose its novelty-value, in time? Is that why men finally simmer down and find a mate, I wonder? Surely even novelty itself must become tiresome after a while.

And really, what is novelty? Most of you don't appear to care for novelty on a very amazing, dramatic scale, I gather (e.g. three breasts, hermaphroditic, etc.) It seems to indicate, basically, "not my usual partner," that much is clear. As in, relief from one's usual partner, suggesting that one woman is apt to fatigue, in time. Possibly it is just that the *wrong* woman is apt to fatigue, since a small percentage of men appear to be entirely and willingly monogamous, or maybe it's that the restlessness that demands novelty proceeds from some other source entirely. I couldn't say. Given that you are expending a lot of effort and/or suffering on all of this, it would not be a bad idea to examine your own feelings on the matter, rather than just being led around by instincts that you cannot control and do not understand.

I am told that one of the principal reasons men like to get married is so that they do not have to go looking for sex anymore: a practical consideration. Finding sex takes a lot out of you (far less, of course, if you have read this book.) Even if men are in a committed relationship, they would still love to have the novelty—"if it was thrown at them," my husband told me.

Thrown, no less! Blasted out of a cannon, or something. It's amazing how y'all really don't appear to have a single clear thought in your heads on this subject.

What would this Strange person be thinking, you know? A new what? Is nothing at all required from the Strange one but bare acquiescence? What is on the other side of the equation? Does it not occur to you that this New One may have thoughts of her own, an agenda, even, and if not, why not? I tried to find out more about this from my husband by bringing up an extreme example, the ill-starred tryst of Bill Clinton and Monica Lewinsky. Sure, she was willing, but given all the complications, the huge risks involved, and the infinitesimal likelihood of a positive outcome for the Strange party to the arrangement, it is difficult to imagine how it all ever even happened. Power is an aphrodisiac, we are told—was it merely that? My husband seemed nonplussed by this question, so I rephrased it: How did Bill Clinton manage to seduce Monica Lewinsky, given their respective circs.? Even if it was Monica Lewinsky who seduced Bill Clinton: what, I asked him, did Bill Clinton suppose that Monica Lewinsky was actually thinking?

O: It doesn't matter.

Me: Surely, he has to at least ascertain, I mean even if she's not in love, doesn't she at least have to be turned on?

O: Preferably.

Me: Ah.

Complicated

One is told that women are complicated, and men are simple. Here is a graphic depiction of this alleged difference that has been widely distributed on the Internet:

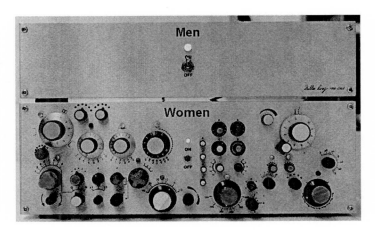

I always found it interesting that women too have an "ON-OFF" switch, positioned in roughly the same place.

If you ask me, the institutionalized indifference to men's complex emotional and/or psychological makeup is a relic of those archaic militaristic societies that valued men for their muscles, not their minds. It comes from a kind of conditioning to respond to orders, to be ready to fight—**ON!**—a type of gender-branding that still persists in most parts of the world. It's every bit as artificial and coercive as the old-fashioned submissiveness and stay-at-home obedience and subservience that have long been fobbed off on women so successfully (and still are, in most places.) But this is in reverse. A diagram that tracks closer to the truth might look something like this:

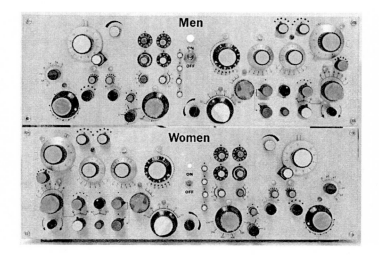

The trouble is that nobody wants to bother about any of the knobs and switches on men, other than just the one. Including men, I believe. All those knobs and switches are still there, though, you have to suspect, gathering cobwebs and growing stiff in many if not most cases.

For proof, let us consider a very obviously multi-switched man, like, hmmm. Practically everyone you know! But for the sake of this argument, let's take an (admittedly) extreme case, the musician and composer, Sufjan Stevens. No conventional one-switch guy would even be an indie folk-rocker at all, but Mr. Stevens piles idiosyncrasy on idiosyncrasy. He has appeared onstage wearing giant plastic angel wings and a pleasantly bland expression. He refuses even to behave like a proper indie folk-rocker; he's terrifically cheerful, is a regular churchgoer, and his most famous song praises the history of Illinois in quite a wonky fashion. When *Pitchfork* made a bit of a bloomer and reported that Mr. Stevens had fathered a child with fellow folk-rocker Rosie Thomas, he wrote them a quite delightful letter, excerpted here:

> "First of all, I would like to thank everyone who called or sent notes of congratulations about the news of my baby. I am so proud.

> "Secondly, the baby is a hoax. I had nothing to do with the baby hoax. I was as shocked as everyone else about the baby.

Such a mighty, mighty man.

"[…] the fact that an internet news site printed a story about my baby without consulting me first is insulting. I mean, it's my baby. Maybe I have things I'd like to say about the baby too. Such as: it doesn't exist."[1]

The question is: is Sufjan Stevens a man? Unquestionably, and a really brilliant one too. Off/on, though? Not really, no, I don't think so. At bottom, every human being is likewise full of peculiarities that prohibit easy categorization, no matter how much attempted brainwashing on this point we must endure.

---

[1]http://stereogum.com/archives/sufjan-stevens-hypothetical-tracklists_002494.html

Anyone, any real person, is similarly full of complexities, potentialities, doubts, contradictions, e.g. *is* a whole, real person.

What we're doing is *oversimplifying* both men and women, all the time. And we oversimplify ourselves too, deliberately, and reason good (or pretty good, anyway.) Men and women both will often gladly trade in their own natural complexity for something easier to run. They go ahead and play to type, do what's expected, don't kick against the pricks, lie low, etc. It's just so much easier to do what's expected than it is to give free rein to one's idiosyncrasies, and then have to go and explain every damn thing to *Pitchfork*. Furthermore, when we take our cues from the group, we can navigate the hive so much more easily. We stake out our place in the world through these predefined roles, as if we were all playing a high-stakes game of Dungeons and Dragons.

Our social institutions really do tend to work out fine most of the time, but now and then the complex creature hiding under the security-blanket of conformity will spring out and assert itself, especially in an emotional situation. Man or woman, this is true. We are all of us more capable of surprising one another than anything on television or in the movies would suggest. It's self-evident, surely. Think of the peculiar cast of characters in your own life, you know this to be true. Not even the genius of a Todd Solondz or a Charlie Kaufman can approximate anything like the real complexity, nuance and craziness of real people.

So men are not really just soldiers, not just muscles, and women are not just empty-headed sex objects. You knew that, I am sure. But just as a default position, just to negotiate our bizarre society, men generally have got a "warrior" component, and most women have a "sex object" one. Meaning, we develop a means of relating to the culture within the confines of those ever-present constructs: if you are a guy you have figured out a way to relate to jocks, even if you're not one yourself. And if a girl, you will have figured out your standard position vis-à-vis push-up bras, high heels and things pink.

This is knowledge you can use to your advantage, tangential as it may have sounded at first. (An aside: I am not trying to suggest *at all* that there is anything right or wrong about any of this stuff, nor that muscles aren't valuable, nor that women shouldn't stay at home, wear lacy lingerie and even literally be subservient, if they want. People should surely be free, and more free than we are now.)

Back to the point, now: I just wanted to be clear that conformity obscures far more than it reveals about real human beings. But knowing *how* someone conforms can be used, too, to predict and exploit what he or she will do or think. And by "someone," I mean this girl whom you are trying to take to bed.

Please bear with me for one more little digression, if you will.

There was a certain look that was in vogue among the young men of the 1980s. Nowadays we look at the poodly haircut and the skinny tie and all that eye makeup and think: "Lawks!" At the time, of course, such stuff looked completely *unremarkable*, difficult though that may be to credit now (and believe me, the same thing is going to happen to the random-tendrilly-haircut and multiply-tattooed young buck of today.) The thing is, though, in the 1980s there were quite a number of beefy bears who really had no business going anywhere near an eyeliner pencil. But because this is what a twenty-something in search of fine company for the evening was *expected* to do, there were quite a number of wholly unsuitable young guys simply sludging themselves in eyeliner in such a manner as to make them resemble a pack of deranged raccoons. Not only could you see *why* they would do this, you could actually *predict* that they would. Since then we have had the trousers falling off, the piercings, the tattoos; the "metrosexuals" and (for the umpteenth time) "hipsters," all in the service of various hopes of seduction, as ever.

Well, we women have to deal with *so much* of this stuff, you would not believe. If you think that the raccoon-faced boys of yore were absurd, what shall we say of their giant-shoulder-padded girlfriends with the radioactive lip gloss, and hair so moussed and tormented that it was in danger of going up like napalm, should a stray spark come too near? Today's persecutions are no less absurd and humiliating. What do you really think of the way we women have to starve ourselves, of the hours we spend trying to look as if we just rolled out of bed, but in just this certain way? Of our neverending struggle to appear both feminine (with all the nonsense that entails,) and competent?

Of course we none of us *have* to do these things, but then again, we kind of do (in the service of various hopes of seduction, as ever.)

All this is by way of saying that you can already understand quite well what makes women tick. Different as we are from you on the outside, we're not so very differently constituted from you mentally. On the outside: yes, of course. The big differences are in the roles we've been assigned by our physiology, by our hormonal makeup, etc. But on the inside, you have the same kind of machinery we do: a brain, an imagination.

So. The very best way to enter into what a woman is thinking, in order to persuade her to do what you would like her to do, is:

Imagine what it would be like to be her.

If you really put your back into this exercise, you will learn a lot. What do you think it would be like, if you lived in the world of women, if random strangers were to start making up to you all the time and asking for your phone number? What would be expected of you, how would you choose to behave? In this weird culture we're living in, would you be very worried about being fat, do you think, or unattractive? If you were a woman, would you get Botox, do you suppose? Would you wear high heels and fancy makeup? What do you think it would feel like to be scared of getting pregnant? Or, can you imagine wanting to *be* pregnant, have a baby grow in your body? How about, what do you think it would feel like to have blood kind of leaking out of you every month?? What would sex be like if you were the one to be penetrated, rather than the other way around? What would it be like to take off your bra in front of someone?

And for the final and most relevant part of our exercise: What would you think if a man presented you with flowers, or wrote a poem about you? What would your position be regarding "casual sex?" What would you think of yourself ("yourself" meaning you, the man, now) as a lover? And finally, the real $64,000 question: would you want yourself as a boyfriend, if you were a woman?

Reflect carefully on all these things, and you may find you know far more about women than you ever thought you did. A lot of times people's bizarre behavior is directly attributable to a perfectly logical cause that would be nothing but evident if we just took that person's circumstances halfway seriously.

The thing is we are *equal*, and our minds and hearts are *alike*, but we are also so very *different* from one another in so many, many ways that it takes a whole lot of awareness and thinking and studying in order to figure out what makes the other half tick. No matter what plans you have in store for the women in your life, it would be a very good idea to understand as much about them as you can.

Like Sun Tzu says:

> *Know yourself and know your enemy.*
> *You will be safe in every battle.*
> *You may know yourself but not know the enemy.*
> *You will then lose one battle for every one you win.*
> *You may not know yourself or the enemy.*
> *You will then lose every battle.*

WHY WOMEN CHEAT

I t's a funny thing, the way we talk about men cheating all the time without really paying much heed to the fact that they have to have someone to cheat *with*. What about these women? Why do they cheat? Is it cheating if they are single and the guy is married? Well, yeah.

I should think so!

Why *do* women cheat? Are certain women more like men than we realize? Do they merely suppose the grass to be greener elsewhere? Is it a dog-in-the-manger thing, where the man is more attractive because he already belongs to someone else? Is it because they are unhappy in their existing relationships? Do even faithful women daydream about cheating, as men are said to do?

Actually no, the answer is: None of the Above.

Really, the Real Answer: Why Women Cheat

This is a big secret. I expect if I could be excommunicated from womankind for telling you this, I would be.

The main reason women cheat is this: no woman can resist the man whom she believes loves her the most of anything in all the world. More than any other man loves her. More than he loves anything, everything, life itself even.

This is such a bone-deep, abiding, eternal feature of womanhood that many of our archetypal models, our most ancient stories, touch on this theme. It appears throughout recorded history, practically. It's true that the earliest narratives of Western Civ. are largely silent on the subject of women's motivations *per se*; Homer wasn't relatively so concerned about how women were inwardly constituted, or what they were thinking themselves. The women in the *Iliad* are practically like trading cards, for all the attention that is paid to their inner workings. But even so, from that early date we begin hearing the familiar tale of women and their fate as the objects of the love and desire of men.

What a number of fine women here
are. and Hoax me, if I saw but two
when I came in. ___ egad I believe I am
drunk ___ so that accounts for it. ___

Exhibit A: Helen of Troy

Accounts differ, but in all of them Paris was crazy about Helen—of everything in the world, he chose her as his prize for naming Aphrodite the most beautiful of the goddesses, and so Helen (and everybody else) was doomed. Paris came and basically grabbed her, and hauled her back to Troy. Then her husband Menelaus had to come after her. The thing is, we aren't really clear on what Helen thought about all this. Paris came, took, left ... and Helen went at least somewhat willingly, it would appear. She seems to feel kind of guilty about her own complicity, if Homer is to be trusted. But really she gave into the ancient imperative, which was that this guy was absolutely not taking no for an answer. So, she went. Result, the launch of a thousand ships, and so on. Fatal beauty ... I bet by the end she wished she'd been born with a hump, or something.

Exhibit B: Guinevere

Now, Guinevere was a good woman. King Arthur was a good man. And Sir Lancelot was about the best man that Arthurian legend has got on offer. The three of them loved one another dearly and thought highly of one another in all ways. Lancelot was Arthur's first, best, most valiant and most trusted knight. But the fact was that Arthur was king, and busy with affairs of state and the

Don't Go to War Over Me Because I'm Beautiful

cares of office and what have you. And Lancelot could not help himself! He loved Guinevere; he loved her more than anything, more than he loved Arthur, more than he loved his honor, more than he loved himself, more than he loved life; and so Guinevere was doomed, and the whole of Camelot along with her.

J.M. Cameron, *The Parting of Sr Lancelot and Queen Guinevere*, via Wikimedia Commons

Bummer! Our Love has destroyed civilization

Exhibit C: Juliet Capulet

Thomas Francis Dicksee, *Romeo and Juliet*, via Wikimedia Commons

This is SO much hotter than *Twilight!*

Juliet, of course, is not an adulteress. Too young! However, there is one thing and one thing only that she is supposed to be steering well clear of, and that thing is Montagues. But let just one ridiculously good-looking young Montague turn up under her balcony, risking everything for a glimpse of her and whispering "dear saint," and boom! Everybody is doomed.

Women cannot help themselves. You know how men can't help themselves about being attracted to women, and wanting them all? Well, women can't help themselves about their susceptibility to being loved. We long to be loved. It must be genetically encoded. Even Margaret Dumont in the old Marx Brothers movies would stop dead in her tracks the instant Groucho started in on her. She might have been about to clock him with a tire iron, but the second he crooned, "Oooohhh, I love you," it was all over, and little hearts fluttering all around in her stately bosom.

Of course, I'm being a little bit flippant here with the fictional females, but think about it! This susceptibility is also present in real, flesh-and-blood women. Women whom you know, who seem perfectly normal and sensible, and then they suddenly go completely deer-in-the-headlights when some man shows up and starts going on about their eyes like stars, skin like velvet, mouth like fruit and all that.

If a man can persuade a woman of his all-consuming love, I mean really persuade her, she will be with that man. If she already has a man, if she loves that man, and another man can come into her life and persuade her that he loves her *more* than her own man does, she is in mortal danger. She is programmed to give her love to the man who loves her most.

I don't use this phrase lightly. Women give their love. This is partly the natural consequence of our anatomical arrangements. For a man to be her lover, a woman must allow him to penetrate her in every way. She actually permits her body to be broken into, pierced. Men will never understand how impossibly intimate this is. They don't experience physicality the same way, and they will never really get it. Because in general, a woman has to make herself so vulnerable in order to accept a lover, she really has to believe that he won't hurt her. It's a form of surrender that contains such trust, and such hope. This is where all the classic tropes relating lovemaking to sieges and gates and battle and vanquishing etc. all come from.

This is to say, the love of women is a gift, is "given," because what we are giving you is our safety, our trust that you won't hurt us. You know how men can sometimes say, "It doesn't mean anything," about sex. Well, you know, I really do not believe that we can do that. There are women who claim we can, but I am sorry, they haven't ever convinced me.

Such women as appear to be very different from what I'm describing here—who don't seem concerned about the strange vulnerability of their own bodies, and are behaving as though they themselves are the hunters rather than the game—might well be asking for trouble, I've often thought, because they just don't seem to be pay ing sufficient attention to the emotional or maybe even spiritual consequences of that ultimate intrusion. Maybe this is just me, but I have seen any number of proud, sassy females brought very low when some man, whom they supposed themselves to have been dallying with for their own pleasure, suddenly complicates matters, reveals his own agenda, stops being the plaything. Maybe he leaves, or he wants to fool around with someone else, or simply refuses to play by her rules, whatever they are. But I have seen it hurt those Amazons just like it hurts the tenderest, most yearning Ophelia among us, and in a very deep place. Nobody can know for sure what goes on inside someone else's skin, but it is patently obvious that anyone can be badly hurt by trusting the wrong person; trust the wrong person to the degree we are talking about, and it can be really damaging, maybe permanently so. However, I am very old-fashioned, and certainly not in a position to be offering anyone advice here, and have wandered off the point besides. Just, it's worth thinking about, perhaps.

Anyway, as we were saying: ordinarily women give their love, bestow it. Just like in songs or poems, they really do. The man comes knocking and we answer the door, or we do not. Sure there are other arrangements that can be made—commercial ones, role reversals, experiments of every kind—but even today, this is the basic structure of courtship. A man comes and lays siege, and the woman eventually succumbs (or does not.) What I am trying to tell you is that we mostly cannot help but surrender to the man who needs us so desperately, who cannot live without us, who will *die* if we don't open the door.

There's any number of reasons, I am sure, why a man might desire a woman so much that he feels like he is going to *die*. One is that she is so beautiful to him that he has become obsessed with her body and feels that if he can't possess her, that is it, life is over. This is commonly called "infatuation," as distinct from actual affection, because it's quite possible to form a very intense attachment to a physically beautiful person to whom we can ascribe all sorts of ideal characteristics without needing to know a thing about what he or she is really like. Even grownups experience a vestigial form of that kind of projection with regard to say, Scarlett Johansson or (ahem) Clive Owen.

There has long been a suspicion that infatuation makes a poor foundation for a long-lasting relationship—I know of several failed marriages that began just this way—but many people, especially young ones, do in fact form long-term connections and even get married on the basis of pure physical attraction, mixed with fantasy.

The trouble here, of course, is that once certain guys have gotten what they want physically, they find, indeed, that they no longer want to *die*, but would instead prefer to live, elsewhere, and take themselves off to parts unknown at breakneck speeds. To be fair, a lot of times it is just not clear to either party where the thing is going to lead. It's not always cynical, when a man finds that thirst is slaked. Maybe he'd thought it never would be, or maybe he was planning to move on to the next unattainable object all the time.

With respect to the question of getting girls into bed with the least amount of fuss—we aren't considering your future here, but you, perhaps, might, because the level of fuss is liable to rise very abruptly, if you don't.

As we were saying earlier, beautiful women like Patsy develop a sort of addiction to the sight of males yearning about the place. Lay the maximum dosage of life-threatened despair on Patsy and you can expect to be heading straight to the boudoir. "He'll *die!*" she thinks to herself happily. "Love, at last!"

Of course, there's another way in which you can be in love so that you think you're going to *die*, and that is when you find someone who makes the world make sense for you. You could call this the Darcy Phenomenon.

Why Women Love *Pride and Prejudice*

Women love *Pride and Prejudice* not only because the clever, brilliant, beautiful heroine of lowly station is rescued by and marries the gorgeous rich aristocratic guy. There are a zillion books featuring this plot that don't attract the type of lifelong, swooning devotion inspired by *P. & P.* What Miss Austen was able to articulate so perfectly in this great novel is the kind of true love enjoyed by what used to be called "soul mates." For those lucky enough to find a soul mate, like Elizabeth Bennet and Fitzwilliam Darcy, the other party is the only other person on this earth aside from himself who does not appear to be obviously and incurably unhinged. Among the cast of *P. & P.*, even the really decent people like Eliza's sister Jane typically exhibit totally irrational behavior that would be unthinkable for our lovers. All the attributes valued by Elizabeth Bennet—brains, a dry sense of humor, good sense, kindness and generosity, white-hot passion kept perfectly in check, etc. etc.—Fizwilliam Darcy possesses in the highest degree. And Eliza provides, for Darcy, abundant qualities—insouciant, quick-witted gaiety and charm, a fierce, proud, utterly undeceived, unconventional intelligence, etc.—that he wasn't going to be finding among the London belles of his ordinary acquaintance. Their love affair is so magical because you can see straightaway that what each values in the other is going to continue to have value, even to increase in value, in all the different circumstances you can imagine them facing together.

This, I need hardly add, is exactly the type of relationship that many, many millions of intelligent, sensitive young women are longing for (so don't even try to wheedle them into bed, for they are not Patsies! They aren't very likely to go for it unless they are in love with you.)

For Men and Women: How to Ensure That a Woman Will Never, Ever Cheat.

Women: If you love your man and I have now caused you to become terrified of having no control over yourself and being just about to fall for any random idiot, the RULE for never cheating is:

Never ever ever permit yourself to be alone with a man not your husband or mate. Don't have lunch with that old school friend, that colleague from work. Forget all about "just friends." None of us is ever truly safe, however safe we may think ourselves. That way, you will never ever be in a position to be listening to anybody telling you how he is going to *die* if he can't have you. Privacy is an absolute precondition for talking such nonsense.

(Hey, what are you doing reading this book, anyway, come to think of it? Put it down at once.)

Oh, very well, then … if you really mean it, and you want to do everything in your power to protect your relationship with your man, make it an ironclad rule never to be alone with whatever guy. It's like insurance. Hang out with whomever you like, but make sure there's at least a third along with you. If some male friend says, let's go somewhere just us—I mean, for years and years I have had absolutely no trouble saying, "Oh no I never go out alone with a man." He will actually be flattered. Maybe annoyed if he had some designs on you, but whatever!! He can be a little annoyed, that won't kill him.

Safety first!

E-mail as a Tool of Seduction.

Now you were thinking about e-mail, weren't you? Quite right, too. E-mail is the biggest threat to fidelity that was ever invented. It is a way of being alone, instantly and utterly alone, without technically being alone at all—free of risk, or cost, or (probably) the slightest threat of detection. Women who intend to protect their committed relationships would do well to go back to cuneiform. Only think what Cyrano de Bergerac gained (however tragically) with words alone:

> *I love thee! I am mad! I love, I stifle! Thy name is in my heart as in a sheep-bell, and as I ever tremble, thinking of thee, ever the bell shakes, ever thy name ringeth! All things of thine I mind, for I love all things; I know that last year on the twelfth of May-month, to walk abroad, one day you changed*

your hair-plaits! I am so used to take your hair
for daylight that—like as when the eye stares on
the sun's disk, one sees long after a red blot on all
things—so when I quit thy beams, my dazzled vi-
sion sees upon all things a blonde stain imprinted.

Yes, all of this and more can now be transmitted over any distance, and instantaneously. No wicked impulse need ever wait on the post, nor even on the time required to dial a telephone, nor suffer the slightest diminution arising from the passage of time, second thoughts, spasms of conscience, a dearth of stamps.

A multitude of relationships has been wrecked through the judicious use of e-mail by some designing interloper. So women who are already attached must take very good care to resist any electronic blandishments they may from time to time receive. The only way, not even the best way but the only way, to do this effectively is to ignore said blandishments and their wily composers entirely. Protestations of any kind will only sink you deeper into the hole, I'm afraid. In stubborn cases you must be prepared to de-friend, unsubscribe, delete unread. Disabuse yourself entirely of the notion that there is no danger in a mere glowing laptop screen fifty miles from the predator in question. Know the computer for what it is: an electronic minefield, chock-full of hidden perils.

Whoops.

My god, what am I thinking? Here I'm supposed to be explaining to you how to sleep with girls, and I go and tell some of these very girls (who aren't even supposed to be *reading* this book) how they should be avoiding your impertinent e-mails? *So*, so sorry about that.

While I'm on the subject, though, you really don't want to set your sights on anybody who is attached, if you can help it, and not only because you don't want to be played like that yourself one fine day. Not only from the karmic p.o.v., but from the logical one, this makes sense. If you court an "unavailable" woman you'll have to talk her not only into going to bed with you, but also into cheating, which is something that a lot of women really, really do not want to do. It's an unnecessry extra hurdle.

I know, it is a bootless errand to go around telling anyone whom he should or should not pursue. The fact that these matters are largely beyond our control doesn't change the score much, though. I promised to tell you how to get laid with the minimum of fuss; I'm bound to point out, then, that the most common cause of fuss is to do with questions of fidelity.

Note to those men who are themselves attached (assuming you've had some success with my earlier advice, here, and that you are now looking ahead to a glorious future with your beloved.) In order to keep a woman close to you, you must take care to be the man who loves her most. Make sure she understands that no other will ever, can ever reach the impenetrable place she has taken deep in your soul, etc. Remind her, once in a while. Remember, communicating this does not require the expenditure of a single cent. It is only a matter of attention and care.

Bonus: Suggested Reading.

Nobody has ever beaten or even really come within miles of John Donne in the manufacture of sweet nothings of irresistible wit and charm, even though the excerpt below was written in the earliest years of the seventeenth century. There is no other writer to my knowledge who so well understood women, so his technique is well worth studying. Here is the master on the subject of his lover getting undressed for bed:

> Off with that girdle, like heaven's zone glittering,
> But a far fairer world encompassing.
> Unpin that spangled breast-plate, which you wear,
> That th' eyes of busy fools may be stopp'd there.
> Unlace yourself, for that (your woman's chime)
> Tells me from you that now it is bed-time.
> Off with that happy busk, which I envy,
> That still can be, and still can stand so nigh.
> Your gown going off such beauteous state reveals,
> As when from flowery meads th' hill's shadow steals.

Off with your wiry coronet, and show
The hairy diadem which on you doth grow.
Off with your hose and shoes; then softly tread
In this love's hallow'd temple, this soft bed.
In such white robes heaven's angels used to be
Revealed to men; thou, angel, bring'st with thee
A heaven-like Mahomet's paradise; and though
Ill spirits walk in white, we easily know
By this these angels from an evil sprite;
Those set our hairs, but these our flesh upright.
   Licence my roving hands, and let them go
Before, behind, between, above, below.
O, my America, my Newfoundland,
My kingdom, safest when with one man mann'd,
My mine of precious stones, my empery;
How am I blest in thus discovering thee!
To enter in these bonds, is to be free;
Then, where my hand is set, my soul shall be.

John Donne, Elegy XIX, To his Mistress Going to Bed

The bed is "love's hallowed temple!" Her body is a "far fairer world" than Heaven itself. Okay!? (And this was a very devout guy, no less than an Anglican priest, eventually the Dean of St. Paul's Cathedral.)

OF CATS AND DOGS

As we are constantly told, all men are dogs, and can be tempted into all sorts of foolish behavior by the merest wagging of the nearest female tail. We are also told that this is the place where women have got men beat before the game even begins, simply because your sex drive is so much fiercer and more implacable than ours. We can control ourselves, generally speaking, where you cannot. We can Just Say No, where you cannot—at least not so generally, nor so easily. It's true that if under the age of say, thirty or so, particularly, you are at a frightful disadvantage. In certain ways, at least; you might crack, give way, give in. Though most commonly women are depicted as wrangling money out of you, lavish gifts, fine wine, clothes and jewels, they may not stop at that. You young, vulnerable

photo by Miro Cacik, via Wikimedia Commons

men, playthings of designing women, who can be forced to do all their unreasonable bidding in hopes of gaining that prize you so uncontrollably crave! Later on, perhaps, you may like to boss and belittle us to your hearts' content, but in the short-term, the power is all ours ...

Wrong again! The truth is that women are really at least as vulnerable as men, because the horrible longing for Ultimate Passion is quite as dangerous as the mere indiscriminate lusting after every woman one sees. Women imperil and even enslave themselves with this irresistible need to be fancying themselves in love. They let themselves in for every kind of deceit; they put up with all kinds of lies, neglect, abuse even, in order to keep the fairytale of passion alive.

But Do Women *Really* Love Sex? (As Much?)

Oh, yes, of course. Many, many women love sex just as much as men do. The sexual impulses of women are relatively super crazy and complicated, though, because they tend to be charged with all this walloping extra current of emotional power and intimacy, as we were saying earlier.

Have you ever seen films or photos of young girls screaming and fainting at the sight of the Beatles in the 1960s? The ferocity of their excitement literally caused them to scream, to weep uncontrollably, and to pass right out in a heap, as we were saying earlier. Men are just not prey to that sort of stuff. If you were to parachute even Angelina Jolie buck naked into a packed-out Shea Stadium full of young guys, it wouldn't cause anything like such a rumpus. I don't think even one single guy would weep, or faint. They might shout a bit, but it would be more along the lines of "Woof" and "Whoo!" and so on, and be really relatively much more detached, un-charged.

So yes, women are brimming with uncontrollable passion too, emotionally, imaginatively derived passion that can be (and often is) readily transmuted into intense sexual passion.

BUT.

Women do not love sex in the same *way* that men do.

Mrs. Robinson and the Myth of Female Predators.

Mrs. Robinson is a fictional character in a famous film called *The Graduate* that came out in 1967. She is played with wonderful sardonic humor by the very beautiful Anne Bancroft. Mrs. Robinson is a rather lonely middle-aged married woman—a mid-20th-century "cougar," basically—who has an affair with her daughter's school friend Ben, played by the impossibly young Dustin Hoffman. Ben enters into the relationship with trepidation, followed by goofy enthusiasm, and then finally winds up running off with Mrs. Robinson's daughter, Elaine.

When the movie begins, Ben is a clueless kid who's just graduated from college, making him perhaps 22 to Mrs. Robinson's 45 or so. He has no idea what he wants out of life; he's kind of wandered back to his parents' house now that school is over, and he is aimlessly mooching from party to swimming pool. His virile-ish young body apparently causes Mrs. Robinson to lust after him (in a rather appealingly jaded manner,) seduce him, and even get kind of a crush on him, before the end. She is all chain-smoking and sexy and full of anger at her dewy young daughter (and eventually, rival,) Katharine Ross.

This MILF, this Mrs. Robinson, is a cherished fantasy of young men; she has reappeared in many, many books and movies since *The Graduate*.

I hate to break it to you, now, but there is *no such thing as Mrs. Robinson*. She is about as empirically viable as the Easter Bunny. Mrs. Robinson is solely and absolutely the construct of a febrile male mind. *Four* febrile male minds, actually: Charles Webb, the highly eccentric author of the novel on which the movie was based; Buck Henry and Calder Willingham, who wrote the screenplay, and Mike Nichols, who directed. Four guys, of course, came up with this idea that a beautiful, halfway sane middle-aged chick would throw herself at *any* 22-year-old boy, let alone her daughter's schoolfriend.

I know this is a crushing blow; I can almost see the sad faces, like so many little boys who've just heard the unpleasant scoop about Santa Claus. But buck up now, *muchachos*, because a little analysis of this story is going to make life on the seduction front a lot easier for you. Let's answer two questions.

1. Why would Charles Webb, Buck Henry, Calder Willingham and Mike Nichols suppose the story of Mrs. Robinson to be a plausible one?

Perceptive as they doubtless were about a lot of things, these four simply made the everlastingly wrong assumption that women are just like men in erotic matters. And what a middle-aged *man* would like would be to seduce a

22-year-old coed, as any supermarket tabloid will attest. So firstly, they were assuming that an aggressive, smart middle-aged woman would harbor the same erotic coed-fantasies that they themselves enjoy (snort!)

Additionally, any four guys would *like* this scenario to be plausible, so they could easily get away with inventing the fantastical fairy-tale of Mrs. Robinson. They liked to fantasize about a gorgeous sophisticated wisecracking older woman seducing their own gauche, randy 22-y.o. selves, I imagine; alas for them, there is no such thing as a BILF. He is another mythical beast.

Finally, during the Cocktail Era, women's motives were absolutely mysterious, not just to men but to women themselves. You can have no idea (unless you watch a lot of old movies, or maybe *Mad Men*) how utterly impossible it was to confront these matters openly in the 1960s. The prevailing atmosphere of total sexual modesty created greenhouse conditions for all sorts of absurd misapprehensions. All of the beautiful, wisecracking middle-aged chicks (the real ones in the audience, I mean) were likely thinking:

"Hmm, well certainly *I* would not sleep with a little boy, and the mere *idea* of sleeping with one of Tina's schoolfriends makes my *flesh* crawl—but perhaps everyone else really does this sort of thing? Am I *frigid?*— Lord, I need a martini."

No, no, Mrs. Robinson is a figment of desire, just like the Handsome Prince. In the movie, you may recall, all our bumbling hero has to do in order to make love to this enchanting creature with the beautiful gravelly voice is basically to stay still for long enough for her to pounce. Which she magically does.

For those who have heard the movie myth that the events in *The Graduate* were inspired by an episode in the novelist Charles Webb's own life: he kept mum on the subject of "the real Mrs. Robinson" for four decades, but finally spilled the beans in the pages of the UK *Observer* in February of 2005:

> "[Mrs Robinson] was an aberrant fantasy of mine that popped out," recalled Webb, 65, a Californian now living modestly in Hove, East Sussex. "I was at home after college, like the character in the film. My father was a doctor and had couples over to the house to play bridge. There was a wife of one of the doctors who came over and at the sight of her my fantasy life became super-charged.

> "I went to the Pasadena Library one day and wrote a short plot outline to get that person out of my system. My purpose in writing has always been to work things out of me. Later I got a grant from my college to turn it into a novel."

> Far from the trembling virgin Benjamin who finds himself in Mrs Robinson's clutches, Webb's youthful passion was unconsummated. "I never said more than 10 words

to her," he said, still refusing to name the person. "On my third or fourth trip through the living room once ... I think she might have said, 'Charles, can you find me an ashtray?' But that's as good as it ever got.

"I'm sure she's long gone. I'd better not reveal her name, because I'm sure her family would be appalled." Asked if Bancroft's cinematic portrayal evoked memories, he said: "Now that you mention it, there was a slight resemblance."[1]

That is the Big Fantasy of men everywhere: *A beautiful woman, not just willing but sexually on fire, who throws herself at me and I don't have to do or say anything, just lie back and let her fly me to the Moon.*

2. But why *isn't* it a plausible scenario?

Why, omg I have been trying to tell you all this time, are you still not getting this?! *Women are aroused by having attention paid to them; by being pursued.* That is how women are constituted internally. It is really very simple but please, let me go over this again.

Women are not constituted like men; they do not, repeat *do not*, become sexually aroused by the sight of beautiful young men, as Mrs. Robinson is alleged to do. They may giggle, they may admire, they may josh their

---

[1] via http://www.guardian.co.uk/film/2005/feb/06/features.davidsmith

book-group girlfriends but really, buying herself a lovely new dress that makes her look fifteen years younger will do a thousand times more to arouse a beautiful middle-aged woman than the sight of all the half-naked young guys you could produce.

Here are four scenarios which will illustrate (again) how this works:

1. A woman takes off her shirt.
   There is a man in the room with her.

   Result: he becomes aroused.

2. A man takes off his trousers. George Clooney, even, takes off his trousers.
   There is a woman in the room with him.

   Result: she waits for George to tell her how beautiful she is.

3. A woman tells a man how beautiful he is.

   Result: he waits for her to take off her shirt.

4. A man (doesn't have to be George Clooney) tells a woman how beautiful she is.

   Result: the possibility of arousal begins to suggest itself to her.

(See?)

If you want a woman to respond to you passion-ately: *you must woo her.* This is, almost without exception, a non-negotiable point. You must admire her, desire her, give her proof that you are longing for her. Then, and only then, have you got even the ghost of a shot.

SEX SLAVERY FOR PATSIES

At last, you have slid in to home plate with Patsy. Well yay, you! We will now assume that you will wish to return thither, at least once in a while. Here is how to keep Patsy on the leash for long, long time. Indefinitely, even.

Having once believed that she has found the one thing she desires above all else—Ultimate Passion—Patsy will fear one thing and one thing only: being found unworthy of Ultimate Passion. This would mainly mean, in the circumstances in which she now finds herself, turning in a less-than-stellar performance in bed. Bed, after all, is the inevitable place where your desperation led, where you

were going to find ecstasy, solace, relief, everything you ever dreamed of, and so on. If the worst should happen, and Patsy does not deliver the ecstasy promised during all that eternal time of waiting, flattering, sufferings real or feigned, expressions of longing, etc., her world will come crashing down in total ruins. That would be like, it looked good but once you had a bite, you no longer wanted any more? Like a dress you bought but took home, and found you hated? Oh, no. Everything rests on Patsy's performance.

And so performance, my friend, is what you are going to get. There will be fireworks on command, pretty much, so long as you can get her to continue to believe in your unquenchable ardor.

What Patsy wants, nay, desperately needs to believe is that sex with her has put, and will continue to put, not only the cherry but the tiny umbrella atop the cocktail of your Ultimate Passion; that it was well worth every tear, every sigh; that the summit of fulfillment has been gained, and then surpassed. In fact, she has spent ages flipping out over the horrible possibility that you might be disappointed in her; that all this heat and pressure and mystery and excitement might fizzle out, in the event. You could call this the Fear of Philip Larkin Effect. He wrote a very sad and beautiful poem about that very outcome that ends in the lines:

... stumbling up the breathless stair
To burst into fulfilment's desolate attic.[1]

So if you want to get P. back into bed, you must make her believe this, that sex with her *was* life-changing, elemental, etc. etc. and that it is just as moving and incredible every time. If you thought she was devoted to you before, just you wait until you lay this intelligence down! She's all yours at that point, I'm afraid. And she is going to be putting a ton of effort into making you continue to say that you believe that she is the most marvelous lover in the history of all women. Now she's committed, now she believes, and if she is *really* paranoid about it, there will be all the trappings you could imagine, candles, massage oil, bottles of that slippery stuff that heats up when you blow on it, furry handcuffs, wacky lingerie with the strategic lacy apertures, the works. If such a girl goes out and buys the furry handcuffs, she is all in on the Sex Slave front. She wants you to wig out every time you even think of her. For Ultimate Passion must be kept alive at all costs.

Maybe you love this sort of thing, so it's all good. If you do, make sure you do your best to let her know how crazy those nurse's outfits or whatever are making you. I mean really, really make a fuss.

---

[1]Philip Larkin, 'Deceptions,' quoted in *The Faber Book of Seductions*, edited by Jenny Newman (London, Faber & Faber. 1988.)

If you want to keep it coming, as it were, you should always SAY you're on fire for her, even when you're not. You're exhausted or don't feel well maybe but even so, you must say it, you're on fire, smoldering at the very least, or will be shortly, because she is the pinnacle of your desire, blah blah. Never let up on this theme, and you'll have all the sex slavery you can possibly handle, all the time.

The Leash

If you are planning to put Patsy on hold for three months while you go off to Edinburgh or something in order to chase down some rival beauty, you are maybe wondering how it is you can convince her that you really are still in the throes of burning desire, because if you were, you would be hanging around her every moment, right? Good point! Fortunately though, from the outset you have cleverly made sure to court and bed Patsy who is, by definition, dumb as a shoe. All you have to do in order to allay all her doubts and fears is (a) make it all your fault that she will be denied to you for some specified period, (b) mourn convincingly and (c) faux-woo her a bit, every now and then. By this means you can keep her on the back burner for ages and ages. Years, even.

She may try to coax, whine etc. in a misguided attempt to get you to pay more attention to her. n.b. Do

NOT get angry with Patsy when this happens. Just don't! If you are ever, ever angry or impatient with her, hide it. I mean, completely. There should never be anything but kindness and willingness in your face, your voice or your body language. Otherwise it will very rapidly become way too much trouble to get her back into bed and you will have to endure a lot of unpleasantness to no purpose at all. Your anger is like kerosene to the flame of her doubts and fears. If you're going to be as cynical about this as you say you are, then you must go ahead and be cynical, manipulative and Machiavellian all the way! That means never letting her know that you ever find her tedious, repetitive, overly demanding, whiny, boring etc. etc.

Do I have to remind you ... what you said was that you wanted to get into this woman's pants. If you're over her, that is fine—just don't call her—simply disappear! She'll be hurt and astonished and all that, but what do you care, you know, you're on to the next thing. Maybe it will teach her a lesson for the next time—yes, it might.

I will go so far as to say that if you really want to be 100% cynical about all this but you aren't a skilled enough actor to pull off the anger-management stuff, just forget even trying to keep this girl on the leash. It's going to be a horrible amount of trouble, seriously, and in the end, I promise you, there will be very little to show for it. And there are far worse risks in store for you, which I am going to enumerate here in a manner which I hope will strike an unholy fear straight through you, right down to your toes. The worst of them is that you might even become so worn down by the endless cycle of guilt and recriminations and desire for sex and "making up" and whatnot that you wake up one day *married* to this impossible female, and then you are going to be SO mad at yourself!

Oh I cannot tell you how perfectly dreary it is to have to be divorced, I really can't. And that is just exactly how it all happens. Don't blame me, I'm just telling you.

We will assume for the purposes of this discussion that you are a very cool cat indeed, one who can handle the leash just fine, as described in the perennially aggravating Stones song, "Under My Thumb." You'll need a good story for those times you'd like to keep Patsy on the back burner while you attend to your other interests.

There are various reasons why it can be all your fault that you must go on hiatus. Work is by far the easiest thing to blame, followed by an invented anxiety, depression, a nameless malaise or even illness, medical procedures, looking for a new job, etc. etc. Be proactive, phone her and tell her you are simply desolate but for the next three months you're going to be knee-deep in this terrible project, etc. Tell her how you're going to make it up to her, using the same special techniques that reeled her in from the first. Your little private jokes you bring up. All sorts of little things you remember about your times together. You remark on a dress you like her in, a restaurant you've enjoyed together. Again, you make it about her rather than about yourself, e.g.:

I loved watching you drink that strawberry daiquiri that turned your lips so pink.

You looked so beautiful that night in the cut-velvet Romeo Gigli skirt that you got at Fred Segal.

(Most definitely, extra points for remembering this sort of detail. It persuades her that you are thinking about her, whether you have been or not. Again, again, again—you can just act like you're thinking about a girl like Patsy, and pretty much obtain the same results.)

Little details like this (and a very little goes a long, long way) will make your parting much more tolerable to her (and you,) even if it is to be a quite long one. If you really want to be sure that you stay in her good graces, send her a little surprise now and then, like in the mail, with a hand-written note. Even one such little attention will keep her on the leash for weeks and weeks (the dumber she is, of course, the longer, as we were saying earlier.)

Remember, she *wants* to believe your every lyin', cheatin' word.

The Really Tricky Part

If Patsy starts to make some kind of noises about being exclusive with one another, moving in together or any of that, you are going to have to be pretty clever to figure out how to get round her without prejudice to your chances for later. Here is one way to go about it:

> *I'm so messed up right now with work, and getting my life solid … you probably have a zillion guys around you, I wouldn't think of asking you to be exclusive with me when I don't have my act together at all yet, not the way I want.*

The beauty part of this is that even if you are a wildly successful man, it still sounds great because you are even MORE ambitious, e.g. you can say your job is so demanding that you haven't got the free time you'd like to devote to her, but you're working on it, etc. until such time as you can be—ha!—worthy.

Everyone, men and women both—we're always making the calculation of whether the effort required to be with someone is worth it. That doesn't stop because you get married, either, not if you've got any sense. You have to be conscious of this calculation, both on your part and on hers. Eventually, maybe, she is liable to kick up a fuss, or you get caught with another girl, or she finds someone else and cuts you off (all of which complications are, of course, well outside the scope of the present volume.)

SEX
AND THE SINGLE MAN

One thing that a lot of people seem to want is to find a mate, a life companion, like a husband or wife. Another is what is commonly called "mindless" or "casual" sex. The conventional wisdom is that women generally fall into the former camp, and men into the latter.

All that is very questionable.

There are men who really do want a mate; there are women who don't want to be married; there are gays, straights and bisexuals and transsexuals and celibates of every variety you can name, every level of promiscuity, modesty. You can make a thousand boxes to put people in,

(OPTIONAL.)

and soon you will find that you've left a ton of them out, and none of the boxes will fit. People really weren't made to be put in boxes, and yet that's what we seem to want to do, is stick them in there.

Marriage is one of the biggest, oldest, most troublesome boxes there is. Sure, I am a fan of the so-called "traditional" marriage for myself but it is actually a specialty container, not for everyone. In particular very, very few young people are at all ready to hop in there.

We are fortunate to live in a time where it is possible to find love and companionship entirely without marriage, and for your whole life, if the box won't work for you. It's quite possible these days to remain unmarried with no stigma at all. So why bother?

Well, because men and women are so different from one another not just with respect to biology, not just emotionally. I believe that even for you, a man, there is far more to this than sex alone. There's an elemental difference that goes right down into our souls, and that difference is uncontrollably appealing, to you as it is to us. We really cannot stay away from one another, can't resist one another, despite all the risk and the hardship.

If we can finally make a real, permanent connection with the other side, if we can get a green card for that Newfoundland, it's like stereoscopic vision for the universe. Life itself becomes 3-D. The long traditions associated with "traditional" marriage provide a lot of valuable guidance as to how to make such an arrangement work, over time. But it's a complicated, demanding thing.

In short, even though I think it's worth it for my own purposes, I would kind of feel like I'm Anthony Bourdain telling people that it's worth learning to become a professional chef. Sure, it was worth it for *him*, but how practical would it be to advise other people to take such a risky and difficult plunge?

In Praise of Cold Feet

Quite a number of men appear to be fairly sane on this point already. If, as it is said, you guys are the ones who are commonly preventing marriage, if you really do want to avoid it at all costs, if you are doing all you can to weasel out of it: I congratulate you with all my heart. The man we could be feeling really sorry for is the one who agrees to be married when he really doesn't want to be. Both the man who reluctantly agrees, and the woman who shoves him into it, are to be pitied the very most. A marriage desired by both parties is the one to have. If you can't have that, Just Say No!

Absolutely do not get married if you feel you are being bullied or even "talked into it." Don't do it!!! Just don't, is all. Please, don't.

So many, many people are going have an opinion about your life, but in this instance the only opinions that matter number exactly two. But almost for sure, her parents will get into it. And yours. Your friends. Her friends. All those siblings, co-workers and exes have got all kinds of suggestions for you, they're all ready to ask when, and where, and things like this, when the topic at hand is so deep and intense, and so potentially toxic, that if they thought about it for a second they would all of them perhaps go very quiet indeed.

I come from a conservative generation and a conservative family, so I know a lot of women who were married far too young, when they weren't ready *at all*. Quite a lot of them were desperate to flee the parental dungeon, and some of them were just plain bullied into it, in rather the same way men are said to be, only by their parents.

An old friend who grew up in circumstances similar to mine (though on another continent) told me that on the day she was married, some twenty years ago, all done up in that frothy white dress and tulle all over her miserable head, all she could think of as she smiled and posed and was made up and lacquered and rouged and primped and fussed over, was *escape*. What a chilling tale. *Turn!* she thought, as she wobbled uncertainly down the aisle of this huge cathedral, hanging onto her tyrannical brute of a father for dear life. *Run! Turn and run!* But she didn't;

she is still married to the same guy, you know, and most unhappily. And her whole life went by like that, just because she did what she thought she was supposed to do.

The exact same thing is what happens all too often to you lot. You permit yourselves to be bamboozled into getting married, every bit as if you were a Patsy yourself, only about *marriage* rather than just sex, which, I should not have to point out to you, is far worse. It is not permissible, of course, but many is the time I have longed to tell some young jackanapes who has gone and gotten himself engaged, *"Are you joking with me right now?!"*

Now, listen to me!

Only get married if you find to your surprise that you actually *love* the idea of seeing this person every day when you wake up. There are a very limited number of individuals of whom this might be true, in any given person's life. Don't be hasty, and don't ever permit yourself to be guilted or bullied into it, because I assure you, you will only make a mess.

I don't say you may not want to, at some point. You may come to want to, and you may not. Maybe you don't think so, now, and that is just fine. All I am trying to tell you is that you must be certain, as certain as you can possibly be or have ever been, about anything; of all decisions, this is the one you have to make with a clear head. Don't get married unless you want to.

But ... What if I Kind of Want To?

Maybe you're halfway okay with the idea, but you're just not completely certain. Perhaps because you've been told that marriage is supposed to be like heaven on earth, and you have been with this girl a while, so you know what it's like; and you are pretty clear at this point that living with this person would not, in fact, be heaven on earth, much as you may like her, and so you feel that marriage now will mean an end to your ideals.

Let me just set you straight, you know. The initial period of lust and so on, that is an animal thing. It's very compelling, no doubt, but it bears the same relation to making a life with someone as, say, composing a symphony does to having lunch. Both accomplishments may feel really good, but your cat is capable of the latter. The head-over heels part is not a reliable guide to how you are going to feel about anything ten years hence.

My mom used to tell me: if you're really in love with the other person, well, then your marriage will have a *shot*. She is right, too. You've got to care for a marriage, really tend it just like a garden, or it will go all to hell.

So, as we were saying: what if you are a guy who has got a comfortable long-term relationship with a woman, you have been going out or living together for years, you have the beginnings of a life together. What ordinarily happens is that the woman will say, it is time to decide. The choice at that point is either breaking up or getting married. And you don't really want to break up; it's a hassle to break up. So that it's not a question of coercion, but of convenience. She wants to get married and she wants to know if you do or not, so that she can find someone who does. If you don't feel so great about it, okay, so maybe you're just not constituted to feel certain, but please know that to proceed from this point without conviction would be wronging the woman in question. You don't want to do that, do you?

Think ahead a little bit. Marriage really can be heaven on earth, but it's the kind of heaven you build yourself, brick by celestial brick, from the sweat of your brow, from your heart's blood. It's an investment, an endeavor. Life has got all these tough elements! Would this be the person you'd want by your side when you face all the aggravating stuff that you are going to have to face, at some point? Do you see yourself as a father, and if you do, is this the woman you would see as the mother in the photograph, etc. etc.? You need to know these things about yourself.

A real marriage is not really so much about the heaven-on-earth thing (which is intermittent, like flashes of lightning that will, in fact, continue throughout a good marriage) nearly as much as it is about the business of facing the world together every single day. Which, if you are lucky and undertake it with the right person, can be the most satisfying thing ever.

Rereading the foregoing, it is all true, but I'm also forced to admit that none of it really begins even to ring the doorbell of the real and mysterious question of companionship between men and women. Mating. Love. It's totally ineffable. For whatever reason, we pair up! We find a mate, we live with this mate, we wake up every day, there he is, I don't know.

So I really entered into writing this book almost as a warning against making a hasty marriage, even though I personally love being married and it is super fun, to me; because it really is just no good even trying it unless you know what you're about, and you're really willing, and you mean to make it work.

These matters are complicated still further by the fact that it is well-nigh impossible to have an ongoing intimate relationship with another person unless it is, at the very least, a monogamous one.

Why "open relationships" don't work

There are some very dumb ideas on this score out there, regarding the temptation to have your cake etc. by having a "main squeeze" and then "freedom" to tomcat around.

This crazy philosophy of "Free Love" is invented anew by every generation, and is quite often tricked out with such pretzel logic as: "I really love you and want you to be Free, so you can sleep with whomever you like," etc. Both men and women have been known to espouse such ideas in quite superior tones, as in, "I no longer need the outmoded ideologies of Yesteryear, I have evolved Beyond All That," and so on.

The proponents of Free Love throughout history, taken together, make for some really strange, hmm, bedfellows: Essenes and Swedenborgians and followers of Aleister Crowley along with Mary Wollstonecraft—the poor kid!—and Bertrand Russell. To this tough old observer, however, it seems very clear that Free Love is nothing more than another wheeze devised by men in their usual hopes of getting into the pants of women. Free Love is like a confidence trick that men attempt to put across by pinning the fig-leaf of a "superior" moral or philosophical position onto the relatively decent, human goal of getting women into bed, thereby contaminating the entire process with an element of selfishness, prurience and coercion that I cannot approve in the least. Broadminded as I may be, I really must repudiate the views of, say, famous Free Love advocate Bertrand Russell, who held that he did not believe he "really knew a woman until he had made love with her." (Oh yes?)

There is a temptation to suppose, given Russell's eminence, that this remark arose out of something more than mere Don Juanism. But really, chaps, that's all it

The Old Goat.

is. It's the male equivalent of demanding marriage as the price of sex. It reduces our immemorial *pas de deux* to the mere duty of an "enlightened woman." It's more or less blackmail.

To try to get a woman into into bed by means of flowers, flattery and chocolates is sporting, and fair, and fun; to try to get her into bed by making her feel intellectually inferior, square or guilty—by making sure to take all the suspense and delight out of it for her—is pure caddishness.

I think it is safe to say that what Russell actually wanted was A New One, and as many of them as he could get (and he was absurdly successful on this score.) Perhaps there are a lot of deluded bluestockings out there who would fall for the Free Love argument, and if deluded bluestockings are your cup of tea, well then I guess it's a good one.

But Free Love does not work, in practice, for the following reason, which is so limpidly plain that the capacious Nobel-prizewinning brains of Russell should certainly have been able (and, I daresay, *were* able) to twig thereto: at some point one of the two Free Lovers will really, really want it to be his or her turn, and the other party will be tied up elsewhere. It just won't do, you see. Love and desire really don't answer to high-flown poppycock of any kind. Or to put it another way, love doesn't take no for an answer. The whole point of having a mate is just that; you've got someone whom you really adore, whom you are crazy about, really, riding shotgun in your life. It's not possible to have that and then kind of put it away when it's not convenient, because the two of you won't be in synch all the time. And the moment you're not, all hell is going to break loose, it's inevitable.

So basically, we're looking at either a casual relationship, or a committed one, like a marriage. But unless you can have a mutual, sincere, monogamous attachment, your relatively casual, classic wooing or "dating" is the way to go.

So ... How to Avoid Marriage

There is going to be a cost for you, here; sadly, you are *not* going to be able to have your cake and eat it too. If you think that Patsy is getting a little too intense on the Let's Move In Together thing, and you don't care to, you're going to have to "man up" as the saying is, and cut it off with her. Find another girl, start over. It is a lot of trouble but in the end it will be *less* trouble, far less, to find and court another girl than it will be to marry one you don't want. And believe me, that is where this is headed.

I know, I know! You don't want the showdown, and/or you are too softhearted to "hurt" (ha!) her. (On the latter point, please understand that from her point of view, being with someone who is just "settling" for her like she is some kind of consolation prize—the silver medal, or even the bronze!—really, you are doing her no kind of favor; you both deserve better.)

Anyway if, out of sheer laziness, you're staying with this girl you're bored with just because she is willing to sleep with you and you've been through all the poetry-writing and guitar-strumming you can stand, I promise you, you are going to wake up married to her, if you don't watch it. You had really best get the hell out of Dodge, if this is how you feel! Don't let it wait too long, either, you lazy dog.

To reiterate for a moment. I know I am repeating myself but I'm so, so serious, now. Have you got *any* idea of how completely odious it is to be in a failed marriage?! You'd be wrecking lives, here, potentially, your own included, if you were to just "give in"; lack of foresight like that is no less crazy and irresponsible than having unprotected sex. That is half the problem with you guys's tendency to let your libido do the talking, you know, you don't *think*. Think! You're supposed to be the logical ones and we are supposed to be the feeling ones, so please, crank up a few brain cells like you're supposed to.

If an honest assessment of your situation reveals to you that you intend to break up, just not right this second, because it should wait until after thus and such a vacation or birthday or Valentine's Day. It's time, right now it's time. Be kind. And keep in mind it's her future, as well as your own, that will come out so much better in the end.

Unto the Breach

So that's it. We've come safely to the end, you and I. I seem to have gotten away with it, too, somehow! So far, no enforcers working on behalf of the Monstrous Regiment of Women have come to break down my door in the dead of night and spirit me off to an undisclosed location. The fact that you are reading this at all is certain proof that I have succeeded in revealing to you all our deepest, darkest secrets, everything you need to know in order to bed women successfully, with no strings attached.

If, as you read this, I have indeed been made away with somehow, please know that it was in a good cause, and I would do it all over again. Because knowing the truth serves us all, no matter how hard it may be to learn it. The truth should always be our point of departure.

And we're not really operating now according to the truth, I think you'll agree. The whole business of courtship, sex, love and marriage has been adulterated with so many fantasies and so much misinformation that men and women alike can spend a lifetime in confusion about how "the Game" is or should be played. If we can learn to operate according to the truth, rather than a lot of superstitious, outmoded "game-playing," things are bound to go much better. I hope this book will go just a little distance toward redressing the many wrongs people have already suffered as the result of wishful thinking, ignorance and fear; maybe it can even help to prevent more pain and suffering, in the future.

Anyway, coming back down to earth, for our farewell: now that you are in possession of these hitherto closely-guarded secrets, what will you do, I wonder? Will you discuss these matters with your friends over a drink or two? (Will you be so kind as to hoist one on my behalf?) Will you fire off an intemperate letter of protest to the author of this scurrilous little volume (n.b. I can be contacted at www.actlikeagentleman.com)? Or will you race to the nearest watering hole in search of a dumb but beautiful guinea pig, in order to test the truth of what I have here disclosed to the Equally Monstrous Regiment of Men?

No matter what course you choose, dear reader, I close by wishing you the very best; not only in your romances, but in all the different areas of your life.

You ought to be all set now, so go forth (but don't multiply! By which I mean, don't go getting yourself blackmailed via the sudden appearance on the scene of some wayward zygote. Make sure and take care of that yourself, okay? Without fail, not ever.)

Well, off you go, then, and sleep with some girls. I'm going to go make tea.

ACKNOWLEDGEMENTS

My grateful thanks to Richard Johnson, Albert Johns, Melissa Conway, Kate Kasserman, Bradley Wind, Randolph Holland, Amy Holland, Christie Mellor, Richard Goldman, Michael Mullen, and Leigh Anne Jones, and to my mother, Consuelo Bustillos, who long ago first hepped me to the facts.

PHOTO CREDITS

Title page image adapted courtesy TheeErin, via flickr Creative Commons

Bell photo on p. 38 courtesy KoS, via Wikimedia Commons

EPIGRAPH (TRANSLATION)

Ye who do not wish well to the proceedings of fornicators, it is worthwhile to hear how they are hampered on all sides, and by what a cruel unrest their slight pleasure is marred, and how seldom they gain it; and then, at what risk, and what terrible pain.

LaVergne, TN USA
20 February 2010
173746LV00005B/6/P